Othello

WILLIAM SHAKESPEARE

Guide written by

Andrew Sprakes

A *Letts Explore* **Literature Guide**

First published 1999
Reprinted 2000 (twice), 2001

Letts Educational
Aldine House
Aldine Place
London W12 8AW
Tel: 020-8740-2271
Fax: 020-8743-8451
E mail: mail@lettsed.co.uk

Text © Andrew Sprakes

Series editor Ron Simpson

Typeset by Jordan Publishing Design

Text design Jonathan Barnard

Cover and text illustrations Ivan Allen

Design © Letts Educational Ltd

British Library Cataloguing in Publication Data
A CIP record for this book is available from the British Library

ISBN 1 85758 841 X

Printed and bound in Great Britain

Ashford Colour Press, Gosport, Hampshire

Letts Educational is the trading name of Letts Educational Limited, a division of Granada Learning Limited. Part of the Granada Media Group.

■ Contents

■ Plot synopsis

The play begins in the Italian State of Venice. Iago, Othello's ensign, is conversing with Roderigo, a Venetian gentleman who, we learn, has paid Iago for some service. It also transpires from the conversation that Othello, a brave and well-respected general in the Venetian army, has promoted a close friend of his, Cassio, to the position of lieutenant. Iago feels that he should have been given the promotion and resolves to bring about the downfall of both the general and his new lieutenant. Iago decides to reveal to Brabantio, a nobleman in Venice, that his daughter, Desdemona, has secretly married Othello. Iago, in order to protect his own position, uses Roderigo to reveal the news. Enraged, and refusing to believe that his daughter would willingly marry a black soldier, Brabantio confronts Othello and demands that he stand before the Senate to explain his actions.

The action then moves to the political concerns of Venice, which is under threat from a Turkish force that is moving towards the island of Cyprus. The Duke requires the skill and prowess of his most skilled general, Othello. Brabantio presents his case against Othello to the Duke, who demands that Othello justify his marriage. Othello does so, and is backed up by his new bride Desdemona, who is called to speak before the Senate. Brabantio is forced to back down: he disowns his daughter and gives her completely to Othello.

Othello is commissioned to protect Cyprus from the Turkish fleet and is dispatched immediately to be Governor of the island. Desdemona will follow him, but they must leave separately, so Othello entrusts his wife's safety to Iago. Iago tells Roderigo, who we learn is in love with Desdemona, that his pursuit of her is not in vain in spite of her apparently happy marriage to Othello. Iago convinces the gullible Roderigo that Desdemona's love for the Moor will soon expire and that he should follow Othello to Cyprus. Roderigo does so and pays Iago more money. Iago decides that he will persuade Othello that Cassio is being over-friendly with Desdemona, and so initiate his revenge.

The action moves to Cyprus, where Othello declares his deep love for his new bride, and orders a celebration in honour of his marriage and the fortuitous destruction of the Turkish fleet in a storm. The watch is entrusted to Cassio and, encouraged by Iago, he drinks more than he should. Iago has convinced Roderigo that Cassio is having an affair with Desdemona and needs to be removed from his position as lieutenant. Roderigo is sent to provoke the drunken and quarrelsome Cassio who, as Iago had hoped, reacts violently to Roderigo's taunts. As a result Cassio disgraces himself by fighting with

Montano, the outgoing governor of Cyprus. Responding to the clamour Othello arrives and dismisses Cassio from his position.

Iago advises Cassio to ask Desdemona to plead his case with Othello – Iago will use this in his plot to make Othello jealous. Roderigo complains that he has still made no progress with Desdemona, but Iago advises him to be patient.

Desdemona agrees to meet with Cassio and consents to plead for his reinstatement. Othello is unaware of this arrangement, so Iago seizes the opportunity to plant doubts in Othello's mind about the relationship between Cassio and Desdemona. Othello allows Iago's words to affect him and breaks out in a sweat; when Desdemona re-enters she offers him her handkerchief to mop his brow. Inadvertently, Desdemona drops her handkerchief which is found by Emilia, who gives it to her husband, Iago. Iago is delighted, as he plans to use it as proof of Desdemona's infidelity – he will plant the handkerchief in Cassio's lodgings.

Othello returns in a state of confusion and incipient jealousy. Iago says that Cassio has been talking in his sleep about making love to Desdemona, and that Cassio has used a handkerchief of Desdemona's to wipe his beard – the same handkerchief that Othello gave to Desdemona as a first token of his love. The poison of jealousy begins to seep into Othello's reasoning and he immediately wishes to avenge the injustice done to him by killing his wife and his best friend. Iago makes a pact with Othello to ensure this happens, and Othello is completely under Iago's control.

Othello meets with Desdemona and, as a final confirmation, asks her for the handkerchief. Desdemona cannot produce the handkerchief, as she dropped it earlier, and she further condemns herself by trying to change the subject by pleading for Cassio. Othello loses his temper and leaves, allowing the other characters to speculate on his behaviour. Emilia suggests that he is jealous for some reason, but Desdemona says that it is probably state business weighing on her husband's mind. True to her word, however, she still resolves to speak for Cassio. Cassio then meets his mistress, Bianca, and gives her the handkerchief which he has found in his lodgings. He asks her to make a copy of it as he likes the design.

Iago continues to poison Othello's mind with jealous doubts to such an extent that Othello falls into an epileptic trance – he now completely believes Iago's false accusations and resolves to kill both Cassio and Desdemona immediately. Othello's deadly purpose is interrupted, however, by the arrival from Venice of Lodovico, a representative of the Duke. While in Lodovico's company Othello can conceal his anger no longer and strikes Desdemona. His actions are met with disbelief from Lodovico, who cannot understand the apparent change in the usually noble and eloquent general.

Later, Othello questions Desdemona about her fidelity and eventually accuses her of being a whore. Meanwhile, Iago prepares Roderigo for the attempt on Cassio's life. Cassio is ambushed and injured in the fight. Iago pretends he knows nothing of the cause of the fight, and when Lodovico and Gratiano enter he sees an opportunity to silence Roderigo – he accuses him of attempting to rob Cassio and kills him. Iago also implicates Bianca in Cassio's attempted murder and orders her arrest.

Othello, thinking that Cassio has been killed by Iago, enters his bedchamber to complete his revenge by murdering Desdemona. He attempts to make Desdemona confess her infidelity, but she continues to protest her innocence. Othello ignores her pleas and mercilessly smothers her with a pillow. Emilia enters with the news of Roderigo's death, and the assault on Cassio, and as a result of a brief revival by Desdemona discovers Othello's murderous crime. Emilia is distraught and cannot believe that it is on evidence supplied by her husband, Iago, that Othello has carried out this most terrible of murders. Emilia pronounces her faith in Desdemona's innocence and vociferously accuses Othello of being a cold-blooded murderer. In response to the clamour Montano, Gratiano and Iago enter. Emilia immediately questions her husband and slowly realises his villainy. In a desperate attempt to silence Emilia, Iago stabs her and reveals his true nature to the other characters for the first time. Emilia dies, and with her final words proclaims Desdemona's true and constant love for Othello. Othello finally understands that he has made a fatal mistake in believing Iago and tries to kill him, but only succeeds in wounding him. Othello asks Iago to explain his motives for such malignant acts of villainy, but Iago pledges never to speak again. Othello's command is then transferred to Cassio.

Othello restores some of his former nobility by asking for forgiveness and by reminding the gathered crowd of the service he has given to the State of Venice. He also requests that when his story is retold, the fact that he loved Desdemona should not be forgotten. Othello's final act is to stab himself with a weapon he has kept concealed, and he dies on the bed beside his beloved Desdemona. Iago is led away to prison as Cassio reflects on the sad demise of a great man and Lodovico resolves to return to Venice to deliver the news of the tragic events that have transpired in Cyprus.

Who's who in *Othello*

Othello

Othello

Othello is one of Shakespeare's most intriguing tragic heroes. He has a considerable reputation as a general and has a nobility that is acknowledged by the other characters in the play, yet he does not command a position of power in the way that Hamlet, King Lear and Macbeth do. *Othello* is a play concerned not with kingship but with a much more intimate personal tragedy, which Shakespeare explores through the character of Othello. Othello's race also creates much tension in the play as, on one hand he is a well-respected and high-ranking general, and on the other he is deemed a less than satisfactory husband for a white Venetian gentlewoman. The prejudice against Othello in the play is one of the sources of his own self-doubt and insecurity which are exploited by Iago to bring about the tragic events in the play. The prejudiced views of Othello, held by Brabantio, Roderigo and Iago, are disproved by the actions and words of the general in the early part of the play. Othello is shown to be calm, controlled, eloquent and deeply in love with Desdemona. His prowess as a general is second to none and he is urgently required by the Duke when the Turks move towards Cyprus.

Why, then, is Othello so vulnerable to the machinations of Iago? Iago himself states that the general has a 'free and open nature' and can, therefore, be 'tenderly led by the nose' to believe anything. Indeed, some of Othello's simple qualities, such as his trust and honesty, seem to be factors that contribute to his tragic downfall. Once Othello is exposed to the intellectual villainy of Iago he has very little chance of survival. Othello is shown to be predominantly a man of action, a soldier who is comfortable with the harsh life and demands of conflict, but who is less comfortable in civilian society. Iago exploits Othello's lack of experience in matters of love, and through implication and suggestion convinces Othello of false 'truths'.

That Othello has the capacity to love is without question, and this heightens the tragic nature of the play. As Iago's poison begins to work we witness the disintegration of Othello's world: he is susceptible to, and consumed by, violent jealousy and he seems to lose all sense of himself. The poignancy of his words towards the end of the play, 'That's he that was Othello; here I am' is palpable. As Othello loses a grip on himself this is reflected in the gradual breakdown of his speech. Ultimately, however, Othello does regain some semblance of his former dignity at the end of the play. His final speech shows a clear understanding of, and repentance for, the crime he has committed and therefore some degree of self-realisation. At the end of the play there is no need for a restoration of order, common to other Shakespearean tragedies, but there is an acknowledgement of an extremely costly and humbling personal tragedy that is made explicit through the character of Othello.

Iago

Iago

If Othello is one of the most intriguing of Shakespeare's heroes, Iago must be one of the most interesting villains. He is on stage from the very beginning of the play and he dominates and dictates the action from then onwards. Much has been made of the motivation for Iago's villainy, and there is no doubt that the promotion of Cassio, rather than Iago, to the position of lieutenant is the catalyst for his machinations. However, it could be argued that Iago does not have a clear plan to bring about the destruction of Othello, but adapts and amends his plotting in response to opportunity. At the close of Act 1 Iago begins to formulate his plans, and at the end of Act 2, Scene 1 Iago decides to manipulate Othello's open nature to imply Desdemona's infidelity, yet his plan is still in its infancy as he suggests that his ideas are in his mind, 'but yet confus'd.' It is not until the end of Act 1, Scene 3 that his ideas crystallise and he decides on the 'net that shall enmesh 'em all.'

Iago revels in his own intellectual prowess and the way that he so easily manipulates other supposedly 'superior' characters. This, rather than other motives, such as being passed over for promotion or the suspicion of Othello and

Cassio sleeping with his wife, seems to be the force that drives Iago. In fact, Iago's villainy and Othello's total belief in his accusations are made plausible by the way that all of the characters in the play perceive him to be honest: Iago's deception is not limited to Othello but even extends to his own wife, Emilia. By the beginning of Act 4 Iago takes positive delight in the state he has worked Othello into and even has the gall to suggest the best way to murder Desdemona.

Once Iago's villainy is exposed at the end of the play he still retains some of the power he has gained by refusing to rationalise his actions. The power that Iago has attained through the use of language is retained by his refusal to confess. Ultimately, although he is imprisoned, he succeeds in his design to destroy Othello and there is something ghoulish about the way he views his 'work' at the end which makes him one of the most haunting and memorable of Shakespeare's villains.

Desdemona

Desdemona has often been described as a counterbalance in the play to the 'hellish villain' Iago. To view Desdemona in these terms is to misinterpret and underestimate her role and function in the play. Predominantly, Desdemona's character is defined through her love for Othello, but she is far from a passive heroine. She is an individual who willingly takes part in a marriage which she knows will be viewed as unfavourable and she is prepared to speak up eloquently to defend her actions. Desdemona is also willing to pay a heavy price for her love of Othello, as she is effectively disowned by her own father, an event she accepts graciously. Her love for Othello is constant throughout the text and her goodness is never in question. It is ironic that it is her natural goodness which leads to her destruction as she relentlessly attempts to heal the rift between Cassio and Othello which is engineered, and ruthlessly exploited, by Iago.

However, the confidence shown by Desdemona at the opening of the play is supplanted by doubts and fears as the play progresses. Her foreboding is expressed through the 'willow' song in Act 4, Scene 3 where, even in the face of irrational jealousy, she retains her incorruptibility. Her presentation in the murder scene is fiercely realistic and harrowing as she vainly attempts to plead for her life. The poignancy of her final words perhaps sums up her character most fittingly. Even in death, Desdemona's love remains constant and true as she attempts to save her murderous husband from blame for the crime he has committed.

Cassio

Cassio is the only character embroiled in Iago's plotting who lives at the end of the play. There is some irony in the fact that it has been one of Iago's objectives throughout the play to ruin the fortunes of Cassio, yet at the end Cassio has leaped from lieutenant to governor of Cyprus. Cassio's courtly manners and his smooth charm are exploited by Iago and used to sway the naïve and uncultured Othello. He is loyal to Othello, and after he loses his position he is keen to regain the good opinion of the general. Cassio is concerned about his reputation and, acting on the advice of Iago, resolves to seek Desdemona's help in restoring him to his former position. He is the perfect gentleman and never acts improperly towards Desdemona. Indeed, when Iago speaks crudely of Othello's and Desdemona's relationship it is Cassio who responds with propriety and respect. However, Cassio's manners and his attractive demeanour are ultimately used by Iago to implicate wrongdoing between the lieutenant and Desdemona.

Cassio is, however, a substantial character and not merely a dramatic device to be used to precipitate the tragic fall of Othello. He does act irresponsibly, albeit with the encouragement of Iago, and drinks more than he should knowing that his judgement will be impaired, which leads to his dismissal as lieutenant. His relationship with Bianca, whose background is dubious, shows that he is more than just a two-dimensional dramatic device.

Roderigo

Roderigo is another of Iago's victims. He is a minor character but he performs a major function in the play, giving us an insight into Iago's machinations and proving very useful in Iago's plans. Iago uses Roderigo to waken

Brabantio with news of Desdemona's marriage to Othello, as well as using him to provoke the drunken Cassio and in the attempted murder of the lieutenant. In addition, the gullible Roderigo is used by Iago as a handy source of income throughout the play. Roderigo can be viewed as a grotesque comic figure in many ways. For example, he continues to believe that, even though Desdemona has married Othello, he can still attain her love and is willing to give anything to achieve his lustful objective. He enters into Iago's villainous plot purely to satisfy his carnal lust and accepts, almost without question, whatever Iago asks of him. The only doubts he has are for his own preservation, and his cowardice is shown on a number of occasions, such as in Act 2, Scene 3 when he is chased by Cassio. He is essentially a pathetic character whose primary function is to provide a means by which Iago can formulate his plans through interaction rather than just through soliloquy. Ultimately, Roderigo serves his purpose and is killed by Iago. He dies admitting his villainy but without inspiring much sympathy.

Emilia

Emilia also plays a crucial role in the plotting of Iago, as she is the one who finds Desdemona's handkerchief and passes it on to her husband. Apart from this rash act, which it appears she undertook to ingratiate herself with Iago, there is no doubting her loyalty to Desdemona. Essentially Emilia is plain speaking (often crude), with a realistic world-view. She defends Desdemona's innocence in the face of potential danger, firstly against Othello and then against her own husband. She is the first character who begins to see through Iago's façade and is ultimately the character who reveals his villainy. Unfortunately for Emilia, she pays for this with her life.

Brabantio, the Duke and other Venetians

Most of the other characters in the play are fairly incidental and are used to give a picture of the attitudes and mores of Venetian society. The Duke reveals Othello's importance to the state by his urgent requests for Othello's immediate assistance in the war against the Turks, and Lodovico and Gratiano fulfil similar roles later in the play in Cyprus, when they react to Othello's apparent decline by mentioning his former importance and respected reputation. As well as adding substance to the image of Venetian society, Shakespeare uses these minor characters to explore themes and ideas in the play. For example, Brabantio, Desdemona's father, raises the issue of racism in his response to his daughter's marriage to Othello. Brabantio, after Desdemona has confirmed her love for Othello, also warns Othello to, 'Look to her... She has deceiv'd her father and may do thee', words which will eventually come to haunt the general. Overall, the limited number of characters does add to the feel of the play as an intimate and personal tragedy.

Themes and ideas in *Othello*

Love

Love

To all intents and purposes *Othello* is a play about the nature of love. Othello and Desdemona are shown at the beginning of the play to be deeply in love, so much so that they are prepared to usurp convention and secretly marry. The fact that they come from different racial backgrounds is a tension that they are prepared to deal with, even publicly if necessary, and in Act 1, Scene 3 they do just that. Desdemona's love for Othello is such that she asks to be by her husband's side at his posting in Cyprus, and when they first arrive the satisfaction and contentment felt by both characters is clearly stated through Othello's words, 'If it were now to die,/'Twere now to be most happy'.

Othello's and Desdemona's love is disrupted due to the villainy of Iago, although the reaction of the two characters to this threat is very different. Desdemona's love is shown to be constant, while Othello's insecurities cause him to lose sight of his love for his wife. As Othello slips into jealousy he loses all sense of himself and his true feelings and reveals his lack of self-knowledge. It is only at the tragic conclusion of the play, when he realises his fatal miscalculations and his misplaced trust, that his love comes into focus again.

Shakespeare also offers us alternative views of love in the relationships between Cassio and Bianca and Iago and Emilia. How do these relationships compare and contrast with that of Othello and Desdemona? How far would you agree with Othello's final declaration that he is 'one that lov'd not wisely, but too well'?

Appearance

Appearance

The theme of appearance is explored predominantly through the character of Iago. From the outset he is a difficult character to define – one can never be sure of the validity of what he says to others because he is constantly manipulating and deceiving. Iago admits to Roderigo that he only appears to be loyal to Othello so that he can get close enough to damage him, 'I follow him to serve my turn upon him...', which is, indeed, what happens. However, the irony is that Iago is also deceiving Roderigo while apparently helping him. Such is Iago's skill that he manages to appear 'honest' to every major character in the play: Othello trusts him completely; Cassio follows his counsel; even Desdemona turns to him for support and advice. It is significant that, once he is exposed as a villain and he cannot manipulate his appearance any longer, Iago ceases to speak and function as a voice in the play.

While Iago can mask his true thoughts and feelings with consummate ease, other characters, especially Othello, cannot follow suit. Iago exploits this by engineering the appearance of Desdemona's infidelity. With some fairly circumstantial and flimsy evidence Iago convinces Othello, whose 'free and open' nature takes everything at face value, that his wife is having an illicit affair with Cassio. The appearance which Iago creates of an illicit affair plunges the play headlong into tragedy and enables Iago to determine the actions of the general.

Revenge

Revenge

Othello is seen by some critics to have the qualities of a revenge tragedy. Indeed, Iago makes it clear at the opening of the play that he wishes to take revenge on Othello and sets about doing so straightaway. He is relentless in his pursuit of Othello and remains as a witness at the end to view his bloody vengeance.

It is interesting that Iago manipulates Othello in a way that pushes him towards his own form of revenge, which will ultimately destroy the very thing he holds dearest. It is ironic that Othello, by pursuing revenge, destroys not only Desdemona but also himself. Iago's revenge is much more pragmatic than Othello's: Iago reacts to the changing tide of events and modifies his plan accordingly, whereas once Othello has decided upon revenge his purpose is clear, definite and crude.

Jealousy

Jealousy is the factor that underpins Othello's revenge. Once the suggestion that Desdemona has been unfaithful is planted by Iago, Othello's personal doubts and insecurities steadily consume him and manifest themselves in the form of jealousy. As Othello's jealous thoughts increase he begins to lose all sense of reason. He accepts Iago's honesty and loses sight of Desdemona's innocence. Othello seems to change both physically and linguistically as jealousy pervades his mind and he loses the heroic qualities he has earlier possessed.

Iago, ironically, calls jealousy a 'green-ey'd monster' which attacks from the outside, unawares, and consumes its victim – this is what happens to Othello. This view of jealousy is also expounded by Emilia as a feeling that is not based in rational thought but is potentially fatal. However, it is not only Othello who suffers from the affliction of jealousy – Iago, through his speech and action, provides evidence of his jealousy of Othello and Cassio, which finally results in his own downfall. Whatever the circumstances, jealousy is shown to be a destructive and potentially lethal emotion.

Politics and the State

The intense personal tragedy of Othello is presented against the backdrop of an equally intense political crisis. The conflict between the private lives of the characters and their public roles and responsibilities is inextricably entwined. Brabantio, wishing for justice when he feels that his daughter has been bewitched by Othello into marrying him, finds himself disturbing an important meeting about an imminent war against a Turkish fleet. Othello, on the other hand, is required by the State of Venice, as its most accomplished general, to co-ordinate military operations, but first has to answer to Brabantio's accusations concerning his personal life.

Once Othello is poisoned by jealousy his political role as the governor of Cyprus is immediately compromised. He loses his self-control and his judgement is impaired to such an extent that he strikes Desdemona in front of Lodovico, an emissary from Venice, and ultimately murders her. Similarly, Cassio allows himself to be manipulated by Iago and also behaves in a way that jeopardises his public position and reputation. While the fabric of society is not directly affected, in Othello the state loses one of its finest generals, and it is with a heavy heart that Lodovico resolves to travel back to Venice to inform the Duke of the tragic events which have taken place on Cyprus.

Race

Othello's race is obviously a source of tension in the play. While he is accepted as a soldier and servant of the state, there is the sense that if he ever tries to integrate wholly into the culture of Venice he will meet with opposition because of the colour of his skin. Roderigo, Iago and even Brabantio, who has formerly invited Othello into his home, display explicit racism towards the general. Because of these latent attitudes, which sometimes break through to the surface, Othello constantly feels an outsider. Because he is different he appears to be susceptible, through his insecurity, to the lies of Iago. Iago exploits Othello's limited understanding of the mores of Venetian society to usurp his considerable standing in that society.

The marriage between Othello and Desdemona inspires mockery in Iago's case and downright rage in Brabantio's, and the fact that the couple are prepared to endure these trials is further testimony to the love that exists between them. In spite of the criticism the two lovers must expect (why else do they marry in secret?) they confirm their love through marriage. The fact that they are prepared to face the possible and probable public outrage only serves to accentuate the tragedy at the end of the play.

Examination

Coursework

Examiner's tips

These icons are used throughout the **Text commentary** to highlight key points in the text, provide advice on avoiding common errors and offer useful hints on thoroughly preparing yourself for coursework and examination essays on this play. They mark passages of particular relevance to the sections on **How to write an examination essay** and **How to write a coursework essay**.

■ Text commentary

The different editions of Shakespeare are usually very similar. However, on occasion there are variations in spelling, punctuation and arrangement of lines. There are many good editions of *Othello* suitable for use at A Level. This guide refers to the Arden edition of the play.

Act 1 Scene 1

Iago and Roderigo inform Brabantio, Desdemona's father, of her marriage to Othello.

The opening of the play is very important in determining both characterisation and audience expectation and, while it is a common dramatic feature of Shakespeare to start the play mid-way through a conversation, it is more significant that the audience is provided with a distinctive image of the hero of the text, Othello. Through this the other two characters, Iago and Roderigo, implicitly reveal aspects of their own characters, too. It is curious

Appearance

that Othello is not mentioned by name at all in the first scene and all the references to him are distinctly derogatory. Iago and Roderigo both refer to him impersonally as 'he', 'him' and 'the Moor', and conjure up a picture of Othello as a 'proud' general who fills his speeches with the epithets of war, who appoints a lieutenant out of favouritism rather than reason and who lasciviously pursues a gentlewoman – hardly the makings of a tragic hero.

It is worth considering why Shakespeare opens the play in this manner, as Othello's subsequent appearance quickly dismisses the false picture created of him. One convincing argument is that Iago's treachery is made

Iago

explicit in his tirade against Othello; his words are seen immediately to be false and unfounded. In addition, it is clear that Iago is toying with the gullible Roderigo, telling him exactly what he wants to hear. Iago's linguistic powers of manipulation are self-evident. Roderigo freely admits that Iago has 'had my purse,/As if the strings were thine...', and our mistrust for Iago deepens after his definition of his own character in lines 41–65.

'I follow him to serve my turn upon him...'

From the outset Shakespeare skilfully introduces elements of doubt into our perception of Iago. According to his speech in lines 8–33 he has been wronged: a lesser man, Michael Cassio, has been promoted to lieutenant instead of Iago, out of nepotism. Iago shows his scorn for Cassio (lines 20–30), suggesting that he has no practical experience of war and that his lack of experience means that he has not 'set a squadron in the field', saying that he is 'an arithmetician' and that he is not even from Venetian society (he is a

Iago

Florentine). Iago complains that his own experience has been totally overlooked, so he remains as Othello's ancient while Cassio, a 'bookish theoric' who 'prattles' without having experience, receives promotion based purely on preferment. It is accepted by most critics that 'ancient' is a corruption of ensign, which suggests that Iago is, literally, Othello's flagbearer. However, Iago's status appears to be higher than this, and Shakespeare is fairly loose in his use of military terminology.

As the play progresses it becomes clear that Othello acknowledges and trusts

Appearance

Iago's counsel, and that Iago is close to and important to Othello. It is worth looking closely at Iago's speech (lines 40–61) as it reveals much about his motivation and character; he blatantly admits he is untrustworthy and duplicitous. He is not a 'knee-crooking knave' who wears out his life in service of another, and he sneers upon loyal servants who do so and who receive nothing for their pains. Iago fits into the category, by his own admission, of servants who appear loyal and faithful but are constantly vigilant to their own gain. Self-interest is the key to his character, and he states this clearly to Roderigo. 'I am not what I am' suggests that Iago is content to hide his true self and his motivation so that he will be able to realise his own plans more effectively. Key words in this speech (lines 41–65) are 'show' and 'seeming' – he is an expert at appearing to be loyal while waiting to 'serve my turn upon him.'

Examination

It is entirely credible that Iago would feel aggrieved at being overlooked for promotion, yet is this a convincing motive for bringing about the destruction of Othello? See examination question 2, page 69.

After gaining further knowledge of his character, how far can we trust Iago's words? Are his descriptions of Othello and Cassio accurate? How far are they disproved by the introduction of these two characters to the play?

Revenge

Revenge also appears to be part of Iago's motivation: he has been overlooked by Othello who, in Iago's opinion, has clearly made an error of judgement in promoting Cassio. Iago is intent on vengeance, and this is made easier for him by his seeming to have 'love and duty' for Othello so that he can get close enough to the general to plot against him and bring about a particular destiny for him. Notice how many times Iago uses the pronouns 'I' and 'my' in ten lines (55–65). He is, it appears, completely self-absorbed and clear in his purpose to bring about the destruction of Othello. However, Iago's unreliability at this point cuts both ways. If we mistrust his view of Othello, should we trust this view of himself and his plans to destroy Othello? Iago is an opportunist; his language matches his audience and purpose at any given point of the play. At this point Iago is predominantly duping Roderigo, with the ultimate aim of causing trouble for Othello.

Notice the overtly prejudicial and crude references to Othello in this scene. He is disparagingly referred to as the 'Moor', which clearly locates Othello's social and cultural background in relation to Venetian society, and then he is insultingly referred to as 'thicklips' by Roderigo. The terminology

Iago

used to describe Othello now degenerates significantly. It is interesting that it is Iago who drives the plot forward: he now directs Roderigo to act and rouse Brabantio from his bed, and even suggests the manner, tone and substance of the outburst – yet more evidence of his manipulative nature and Roderigo's compliant foolishness. Iago seems to delight in the fact that Brabantio's comfortable existence is about to be poisoned by the news they are to divulge to him, and his control is firmly established by the number of imperatives he uses in his speech (lines 67–73): he orders Roderigo to 'call-up', 'rouse', 'make after', 'poison', 'proclaim', 'incense', ' plague' and 'throw'. Linguistically, Iago is determining the action once again. Notice how he hijacks Roderigo's reasonably polite and ineffective attempts to rouse Brabantio by throwing in the concept of theft. Iago echoes the word 'thieves' five times, and associates the term not only with Brabantio's material possessions, but also with his daughter Desdemona.

'What is the reason of this terrible summons?'

Brabantio's rude awakening is exacerbated by Iago's continuation of the theft image which he specifically links, metaphorically, to the Signor's daughter, Desdemona. The explicit image of Othello as 'a black ram tupping' Desdemona, the 'white ewe', is loaded with racist connotations, and black is implicitly linked to evil as Iago suggests that the 'devil', Othello, will father Brabantio's grandchildren if he is not stopped. Remember that, at this point, Brabantio is unaware of what is happening or that Othello is the culprit who has so crudely stolen his daughter. Iago cleverly fuels the fire of Brabantio's wrath by talking in suggestive riddles. Indeed, Brabantio's initial reaction is that he has been woken by madmen. Iago now slinks into the background, and it is significant that Roderigo steps from the shadows and reveals his identity while Iago remains hidden. Is this another reason to question Iago's motives and character? It is also noteworthy that once Roderigo takes sole responsibility for talking to Brabantio the warnings lose their intensity. Brabantio recognises Roderigo as a pest who has been constantly moping around his residence in pursuit of Desdemona. Brabantio suggests that Roderigo is drunk and full of bad feeling because he cannot marry Brabantio's daughter. Roderigo loses the initiative as he attempts to speak with Brabantio, saying 'Sir, sir, sir,' and asking for 'Patience, good sir...'. Just as the impetus seems to be lost and Roderigo desperately suggests that his intentions come from a 'simple and pure soul', Iago bursts into the scene once again with crudely direct accusations that cannot be ignored.

Examination

However distasteful we might think Iago's words are, his skill as a manipulator is clearly evident. See examination question 2, page 69.

Up to this point the dialogue has been conducted in socially polite and acceptable blank verse, which reflects the status of the characters in the play; Iago now changes the rubric and speaks to Brabantio in prose. It could be argued that the reason for this is that Iago is attempting to regain the initiative lost by Roderigo and so speaks plainly to wrest back Brabantio's attention; the subject matter and the language and imagery used by Iago become even more sordid. He again uses an animal image to describe Othello, suggesting bestiality, and forces Brabantio to pay attention to the news that the Moor (the first time a reference to Othello has been made to Brabantio) is making the 'beast with two backs' with his beloved daughter. Iago's bluntness and shocking imagery allow Roderigo the opportunity to relate to Brabantio the elopement of Desdemona with Othello.

Once again notice the negative associations that Roderigo attributes to

Appearance

Othello: he is a 'lascivious Moor' who is 'extravagant' and 'a wheeling stranger/From here, there and everywhere.' Roderigo makes the point here that Othello is not from Venetian society, a point that transpires to be a key concern of Othello's throughout the play. Othello constantly feels he has to prove that he is civilised and polite and that his colour and race do not exclude him from civility. It is significant that Roderigo talks of manners, civility and reverence when referring to Desdemona's revolt that has been inspired by the Moor.

'I must show out a flag, and a sign of love,/Which is indeed but sign.'

It is significant that, once Brabantio accepts the plausibility of Roderigo's account and is stirred into action, calling for light, Iago disappears into the shadows. He tells Roderigo that the time is not right for him to be seen openly and publicly against Othello. Othello's importance to the state is shown clearly here. The Moor has already been commissioned to duty in the war against the Turks, and Iago is shrewd enough to know that this incident and accusation is not enough to bring about the disgrace of Othello. Is Iago shown to be pragmatic here, or just wilful? He has roused Brabantio and seems to relish the trouble he has caused and, in line 154, he repeats that he hates Othello. There is some irony in the fact that Othello's ensign is to bear a false show of his own feelings: the sign and flag motif runs throughout the play. Iago's final act in this scene is to give away the whereabouts of his general, and he sneaks off to join him in readiness for the arrival of Brabantio and his entourage.

Iago

Brabantio's reaction to the discovery that his daughter has secretly left the house makes him think the worst and he descends into a dialogue with himself at the same time as speaking with Roderigo. This shows his emotional turmoil, and the use of parenthesis and exclamation further reveals his distress and anger. It is interesting that Brabantio views Desdemona's actions as betrayal and, when Roderigo confirms that Othello and Desdemona have probably married, he is enraged and searches for reasons behind her actions. It is worth noting that Brabantio's anger is natural and expected in the context of the times – Desdemona has gone against social conventions in secretly marrying Othello, even though she gives eloquent reasons for her actions in Act 1, Scene 2, and the audience can empathise with Brabantio's reaction. Brabantio then suggests that the reason for Desdemona's apparent betrayal could have something to do with a 'charm', obviously administered by the foreigner Othello, which has in some way poisoned Desdemona's mind and made her behave unnaturally. This idea seems to germinate in Brabantio's mind as it surfaces more vehemently in Act 1, Scene 2. Armed and enraged, Brabantio and his men set off to look for Othello, guided by Roderigo.

Act 1, Scene 2

Iago warns Othello of Brabantio's state of mind and imminent arrival. Cassio brings a message from the Duke of Venice calling Othello to a council of war. Brabantio and his party arrive – a conflict is avoided, but Brabantio is to accompany Othello to the meeting with the Duke, and promises to raise the issue of the secret marriage.

Iago

Here we see Iago's performance of the faithful servant as he relates to Othello his amended version of the night's events. The dramatic irony of this scene is self-evident as Iago gives a wholly inaccurate version of his loyalty to Othello. He falsely describes how, on hearing his master's good name slandered, he has almost been driven to commit murder, inhibited only by his virtuous nature. Once again Iago's villainy, which is cleverly concealed from his fellow characters, is made explicit to the audience and heightens the initial dramatic tension. Iago does not miss the opportunity to provoke Othello and implies that Brabantio is a powerful man and has the popularity and potential to dissolve the marriage between the general and Desdemona.

Our first view of Othello

A picture of Othello has already been drawn in the opening scene by both

Othello

Iago and Roderigo, but it is not until this the second scene that the audience finally meet Othello for themselves. The negative image of the Moor built up by Iago is, to a certain extent, disproved by Othello's first comment in the play which is conciliatory rather than bombastic. In response to Iago's false lament that he should have attacked a villain who was besmirching the good name of Othello, the general states, ' 'Tis better as it is.' However, it is clear that Othello is aware of his importance to the State of Venice, and the pride that Iago has mentioned previously emerges in his next speech. Othello shows himself to be pragmatic as he acknowledges that the Duke's need for his skills as a general will outweigh the complaints of Brabantio. His confidence is demonstrated further when, believing that Brabantio and his men are approaching, he is determined to directly defend his decision to marry Desdemona. His natural abilities, his title and his inner confidence present us with an impressive figure.

Love

Othello's deep love for Desdemona is obvious. Not only have they married secretly, against social convention, but Othello is now determined to ensure the marriage will not be put in any jeopardy. His love for Desdemona and his marriage to her cannot be traded for all the treasure in the sea, regardless of who disapproves of the match. Why is it important, at this point, that the audience is convinced of Othello's true love for Desdemona?

The dramatic tension is heightened by the arrival, not of Brabantio and his men, but of Cassio, Othello's newly appointed lieutenant, with soldiers of the Duke. Cassio brings a message from the Duke summoning Othello, confirming Othello's prowess as a general and his importance to the State of Venice.

Cassio's importance to Othello is made clear as soon as he has finished speaking, when Othello states ' 'Tis well I am found by you.' The short conversation between Cassio and Iago that follows is interesting and raises some questions: Cassio asks Iago why Othello is staying at this particular place and, when Iago reveals that Othello is married, Cassio asks to whom. This is strange as, later in the play, we find out that Cassio has acted as Othello's go-between in his wooing of Desdemona. Perhaps, as some critics suggest, Cassio here pleads ignorance so as to stay loyal to Othello and not to betray his confidence. Would you agree with this suggestion?

Iago

Iago skilfully raises the tension further by warning Othello that Brabantio comes with 'bad intent'. When Brabantio and his men make their belligerent entrance Iago cunningly singles out Roderigo to fight with: if there is to be a fight Iago would not want Roderigo to be hurt as this would be financially costly to him; in addition, Iago knows that he will not be hurt by his secret ally; finally, he can show his false loyalty to Othello by being prepared to fight for him in this matter of honour.

In the midst of a potential disaster it is Othello who acts graciously and is once again conciliatory rather than hot-headed. He attempts to diffuse the situation by asking for peace and acknowledging his respect for Brabantio. In contrast, Brabantio shows much less control, reflecting his emotional state. He has already referred to Othello as a thief and he does so again with added aggression: 'O thou foul thief, where hast thou stow'd my daughter?'

Brabantio's verbal assault on Othello shows some revealing ideas, not only about Brabantio's character, but also about views held by society in general. Brabantio's problem is not so much that Desdemona has married, but that she has married a black general. Brabantio suggests that Othello must have 'enchanted' Desdemona with magic, charms and with various potions and drugs, and he attacks Othello's integrity and race. He suggests that Othello has corrupted his daughter and has married her against her will. Note the contrast here between the language used by Brabantio when describing Desdemona – 'tender', 'fair', 'happy' and 'delicate youth' – and the language used to describe Othello – 'foul thief', 'damn'd'. Ultimately, Brabantio's tirade against Othello confirms to the audience that Othello is not an integral part of Venetian society: even though he is a renowned soldier and servant of the state there is some reticence to accept him fully. While it could be argued that Brabantio is a spurned father, a man whose pride has been injured and who has felt a social injustice, and thus that his reaction is understandable, beneath the personal attack more common and general prejudices against the Moors as a race are revealed. Do you have any sympathy for Brabantio's viewpoint, or do you think his disapproval reflects a deep-rooted racism?

'Were it my cue to fight, I should have known it...'

Look at the way Othello handles this potentially volatile situation with confidence, authority and a touch of arrogance. He graciously keeps the peace once more, but states that it is under his terms, asking Brabantio where he would like the charges that he has brought against Othello to be answered. Notice the eloquence of Othello's speech, the fluency of which reflects his control of the situation. Contrast this with Brabantio's reply, which is broken with commas and, later, with short rhetorical questions that suggest he has no control over the events that are unfolding. How do you view Othello at this point in the play?

Othello

Othello counters Brabantio's demand for imprisonment by telling Brabantio that the Duke is in council and requests Othello's services, confirming his immediate and real importance to the state in this time of conflict. Undeterred, although surprised by Othello's news, Brabantio determines to visit the Duke with Othello and is confident that he will be dealt with judiciously, and that the Duke will give time to his domestic concerns in spite of the political problems.

Examination

Othello's reaction to Brabantio's accusations provides plenty of evidence to prove that Othello is, indeed, a character who can be calm, controlled and confident. See examination question 1, page 68.

Act 1, Scene 3

Othello defends his secret marriage to Desdemona, and she confirms his story. Brabantio disowns his daughter. Othello and Desdemona are sent to Cyprus in anticipation of an attack by the Turks. Roderigo follows the couple to Cyprus after being convinced by Iago that he will bring about the downfall of Othello and that Roderigo will attain Desdemona.

A council of war

The scene now changes from the very domestic problems of Othello to the public problems of state. The Duke of Venice, together with important Senators, is discussing the information coming in regarding the hostile Turks. The scene is given a heightened dramatic tension by the constant interruption by messengers bringing different or changing news of the situation. The picture that gradually builds up of a hostile fleet of Turkish ships bearing down upon Cyprus suggests that conflict is imminent. However, in this section Shakespeare implicitly touches upon another theme of the play – treachery.

Appearance

As the fast-flowing and divergent news of the Turkish force becomes clear, so does the guile and military plotting. One report suggests that the Turkish fleet is heading for Rhodes, which seems to be an island of much less strategic importance or concern to the Venetians. The first Senator is sceptical of the motives of the Turks, suggesting ''tis a pageant,/To keep us in false gaze...', and he is proved right when the next messenger confirms that a Turkish fleet has headed towards Rhodes only to meet up with additional ships and change its course back to Cyprus.

Othello

At this dramatic point in the scene, when the intent of the Turkish fleet is clear and war is unavoidable, the Duke's council welcomes the arrival of Othello and Brabantio. Notice how it is Othello who is greeted first and that the Duke's perception of Othello's character is that he is valiant. His address to Brabantio seems at worst an afterthought, at best slightly awkward as the Duke suggests that he has 'lacked [Brabantio's] counsel and [Brabantio's] help tonight'. Remember that messengers, including his own lieutenant, have been looking for Othello all night. In this time of crisis who is more important to the Duke, Brabantio or Othello?

Brabantio's dramatic build-up to the revelation that Othello has 'stolen' his daughter propels domestic concerns right into the heart of government. Brabantio colours his accusation, once again, with the suggestion that his daughter has been the victim of charms and spells, which could be construed as an attack on Othello's race, although he does not at first reveal Othello's name.

The dramatic irony here is irresistible. Just as the Duke, who obviously has great need of Othello, states that the man responsible for Brabantio's grief will have to face the consequences of his actions and face the 'bloody book of law' to the 'bitter letter' Brabantio reveals to the Duke that the man in question is Othello.

'Rude am I in my speech...'

Othello's account, or defence, of how he has wooed Desdemona now begins. This is his first major speech and he shows himself to be an eloquent speaker.

Othello

He is courteous and deferential, admitting that he has 'ta'en away' Brabantio's daughter, but saying that the only crime he has committed is that of marriage. Othello suggests that he is not a man of words but a soldier, and ironically claims that he is rude in speech and will damage his case by trying to defend his actions verbally. What we then hear is far from the crude speech Othello would have us believe is all he is capable of. His speech is well-crafted and mannered as he respectfully bids for patience from his illustrious audience to hear his tale. It is interesting that Othello cleverly echoes and mocks the words of Brabantio by saying he will gladly share the manner in which he has drugged, charmed and used magic to win Desdemona.

Examination

Many critics feel that even in his eloquence Othello cannot help but betray his pride. Before he asks permission to defend his actions he mentions his feats in battle and his service in the field of conflict. Is Othello wallowing in his own pride here, or does he mention his heroics in battle for any other reason? See examination question 1, page 68.

As with Othello at the beginning of the play, the audience is given specific

Desdemona

views of Desdemona before she enters the action. Brabantio has already implied that she has been an innocent, passive victim of Othello's charms, and here he restates that she has never been 'bold of spirit' and that it is inconceivable that she would fall in love with Othello. Brabantio sees the union as unnatural and reiterates that he feels that there has been some devilry at work. Does the description of Desdemona as a shrinking violet match with your impression of her when she subsequently enters the play? Does she come across as a passive character who is an unequal partner in love?

As the impromptu trial continues Othello shows confidence in

Love

Desdemona's love for him when, in response to a question from one of the Senators gathered, he requests that Desdemona be sent for to confirm his story. Such is the depth of Othello's trust and love for Desdemona that he is prepared, if Desdemona should speak against him, to lose not only his office but also his life. This is a dramatic statement, the intensity of which is increased as the Duke dispatches two of his attendants to fetch Desdemona. Othello's trusting nature is exposed here as a strength, yet also, forebodingly, as a weakness. Othello's trust in Iago to find his wife is loaded with dramatic irony as the audience has seen the contempt and hatred that Iago feels for Othello.

Othello then tells of how the love between he and Desdemona has blossomed. Othello recalls that, ironically, he had met Desdemona when Brabantio invited him to his house and questioned him about his military exploits and adventures. Othello's skill as a speaker is shown again as he relates the remarkable story of his life, which has included great heroism in battle, capture, then slavery, and his subsequent travels and meetings with cannibals and strange peoples. Desdemona had listened to Othello's storytelling and gradually, through pity, fallen in love with him. The only 'witchcraft' Othello claims he used to woo Desdemona was the epic story of his life: 'She lov'd me for the dangers I had pass'd,/And I lov'd her that she did pity them.' Othello, at this point, is absolutely confident of Desdemona's love and he knows that she will confirm his story of how they fell in love. The Duke's reaction is significant here as he concedes that the 'tale' he has just heard would win his daughter's love too. What is your view of the manner in which Desdemona and Othello fall in love? Their love, it appears, has grown gradually. What does this suggest about Iago's claims, later in the scene, that the relationship is based on lust rather than love? What is your reaction to the Duke's response? Is he genuinely impressed by Othello's story or does he see the tale as being an expedient way of clearing Othello of any wrongdoing so that they can focus again upon affairs of state? The testimony of Desdemona takes on added importance as you consider some of these issues.

Examination

There is no doubt that Othello, here, is taking a risk. The Duke could effectively annul his marriage to Desdemona and imprison him. It is clear that at this point the most important thing in Othello's life is his love for Desdemona. See examination question 1, page 68.

Desdemona

The dramatic impact of Brabantio's words before Desdemona speaks intensifies the scene, as he suggests that destruction should befall him if his daughter has in any way 'half the wooer'. He then asks Desdemona to state where her obedience lies, with her father or with Othello. Desdemona's reply is reminiscent of Cordelia's in *King Lear*. Duty and obedience to a father were expected and unquestioned at the time, and the father would have had complete control over his daughter. Now that Desdemona is married, however, her loyalties are divided and she feels the greater loyalty to her husband. This is a great test not only of Desdemona's love but also of her nerve. She acknowledges her gratitude and love for her father but admits that she cannot give him all her love as she now has a husband who is foremost in her affections.

The speech Desdemona makes in lines 180–189 shows that she is a fiercely independent character. She does not hesitate to declare her love for Othello publicly. The whole of this speech provides good evidence of Desdemona's credibility as a character (see the coursework question on page 64).

Coursework

Brabantio is deflated by the words of Desdemona, and immediately disowns her and offers her to Othello. Seeing that he no longer has a claim over his daughter he urges the Duke to return his attention to the military threat of the Turks. It is significant that here the Duke attempts to heal the obvious rift between father and daughter and tries to offer objective advice to Brabantio. The Duke's 'sentence' is in rhyming couplets, a dramatic device often used to suggest a character is to conclude speaking upon a particular matter: it will be his last word on the issue and therefore the advice is to be listened to. Still Brabantio is unmoved and swiftly, perhaps too swiftly, the Duke turns his attention to matters of war. The distinction between the personal and the public is again emphasised in the change from blank verse to prose. The time for ceremony has gone, the details of the imminent war must be spoken of quickly and crudely. The use of prose by the Duke changes the tempo of the scene and adds an urgency to the matters at hand. The Duke reveals his plan to dispatch Othello to Cyprus to defend the island against the Turks. What does the Duke's decision suggest about his evaluation of Othello as a soldier?

Othello shows that he is at his best when he is involved in military affairs:

Love

he is primarily a soldier and he loves his profession. In spite of the fact that he has only just married he accepts the wishes of the Duke dutifully and with some relish. It is significant that Othello asks the Duke to ensure that Desdemona is cared for while he is away. The question of Desdemona staying at Brabantio's is disputed, and the rift between father and daughter is now complete. Desdemona beseeches the Duke to allow her to travel with Othello on his expedition to Cyprus. Her love has been born, she argues, from the tales he has told about himself as a man of action and so she would like to see him realising the role that initially won her heart. Othello supports Desdemona's plea and reassures the Duke that he will not neglect his duties to the state, suggesting that his relationship with Desdemona has a depth which transcends purely sexual gratification: the presence of Desdemona, rather than being a distraction, would be a benefit to Othello. Is the audience supposed to be convinced that the couple love each other deeply? Ironically, Othello suggests that if his personal life did affect his judgement he would accept his downfall and expect to lose his reputation. The Duke shows complete confidence in Othello's judgement and leaves the final decision in his hands. The imminent threat of the Turks means that Othello, his men and now Desdemona are required to leave for Cyprus immediately.

'She has deceiv'd her father and may do thee.'

Brabantio's parting words to Othello, as the council disperses, resonate throughout the rest of the play. The theme of sight and seeing beneath the surface to the real person is also touched upon by Brabantio. This is quite significant, as Othello addresses Iago immediately afterwards. Othello views Iago as a loyal servant – he has no need to doubt that he is anything other than this.

Appearance

With dramatic irony, Othello addresses him as 'honest Iago', and will do so on numerous occasions after this. Othello trusts Desdemona's faith with his life, and in the same sentence declares his absolute trust in Iago. Care of Desdemona and her safe passage to Cyprus are left in the hands of his 'honest' servant. Othello also instructs Iago to arrange for his own wife, Emilia, to attend on Desdemona.

Iago and Roderigo are now left alone, and an almost tragi-comic scene ensues. Roderigo's world has been destroyed: the attempt to discredit Othello has backfired and the union between Othello and Desdemona is stronger than ever. Roderigo's woeful laments that he is about to drown himself are darkly comic as Iago skilfully convinces him that he still has a chance to attain Desdemona's love. Iago reveals his low opinion of the female sex, referring derogatorily to Desdemona as a 'guinea-hen' and suggesting that no woman is worth suicide. He pours scorn on Roderigo's defeatism, and says that love is merely a small part of the greater whole, which is lust. It is worth noting that the dialogue slips into prose again as Iago advises Roderigo to go to Cyprus and bide his time there until the 'love' of Othello and Desdemona fails. Iago talks about the destruction of Othello and his commitment to bringing this about, but his real skill as a manipulator, which is disturbingly comic, is the way he repetitively commands Roderigo to 'Put money in thy purse'. No less than nine times in the space of approximately forty lines (340–380) Iago urges Roderigo to fill his purse with money and journey with him to Cyprus. Roderigo is duped, but the audience is not, as Iago confirms his manipulation of Roderigo with the line 'Thus do I ever make my fool my purse'. This confirms our suspicions from the opening scene that Iago is only using Roderigo to embezzle money from him and that Roderigo, blinded by lust and stupidity, falls easily into Iago's trap.

'When she is sated with his body, she will find the error of her choice.'

Love

Iago convinces Roderigo that Othello and Desdemona are not in love and that their lust for one another will soon be satisfied. He plays on the fact that Roderigo is a Venetian and thus, by that fact alone, more desirable than the 'barbarian' Othello. It is clear from Iago's words that, ironically, it is Roderigo's feelings that are based on lust not love. Iago talks of Roderigo eventually 'enjoying' Desdemona, and of the pleasure that both he and Roderigo will derive from 'cuckolding' Othello. What aspects of Iago's character are revealed here?

Examination

Iago's manipulation of Roderigo is grotesque yet exemplary. From the beginning of the play to the very end Iago controls Roderigo with ease. This scene is just one of many examples of Iago's skill. See examination question 2, page 69.

Iago

Iago's soliloquy at the end of this scene confirms his villainy and reveals his sneering contempt for Roderigo. He goes on to 'engender' his plan to overthrow Cassio and, in the process, damage Othello whom he 'hates'. Iago almost inadvertently throws into the speech a suspicion that Othello has slept with Emilia, his wife, but this groundless accusation is altogether unconvincing as an explanation of his hatred of Othello. It is apparent that it is the promotion of Cassio rather than himself which rankles with Iago, and it is with this in mind that he begins to formulate a plan to wreak havoc. He intends to take advantage of the 'free and open nature' of Othello by accusing Cassio of being too familiar with Desdemona and implying that their relationship is improper. Cassio has a 'smooth dispose' and is handsome, 'fram'd to make women false', giving Iago's story some credibility. There is heavy irony in the way that Iago deconstructs Othello's character as being too trusting, 'That thinks men honest that but seem to be so', and in the way that he will use Othello's trust in him to bring about his downfall. Iago seems to take delight in his machinations, and the act ends dramatically with Iago calling upon hell and dark powers to bring his scheme to fruition. Some critics suggest that Shakespeare's characterisation of Iago is melodramatic here and his reasons for bringing about the downfall of Othello are rather arbitrary. Do you agree? Is Iago presented simply as an evil opportunist or does he have reason to feel aggrieved?

■ Self-test questions Act 1

Who? What? Why? When? Where? How?

1 Who says 'I follow him to serve my turn upon him...', and why is this significant?
2 What devices does Iago use to stir Brabantio into action?
3 Why has the Duke sent for Othello?
4 When, according to Othello, did he win the heart of Desdemona?

5   Where is Othello sent to by the Duke and why?
6   How old is Iago?
7   Who is referred to as 'A man he is of honesty and trust', and why is this ironic?
8   What, at the end of Act 1, does Iago promise Roderigo he will do for him?
9   From where does Cassio originate?
10 When does Iago first soliloquise and what is revealed through this speech?

Who said this, and why?
1   'I think this tale would win my daughter too...'
2   'O thou foul thief, where hast thou stow'd my daughter?'
3   'Even now, very now an old black ram/Is tupping your white ewe.'
4   'Rude am I in speech...'
5   'I do perceive here a divided duty...'
6   'I ha't, it is engendered.'

Prove it!
Provide comment and textual evidence to prove the following statements.
1   Othello is important to the State of Venice.
2   Othello has complete faith in Desdemona's fidelity.
3   Iago hates Othello.
4   Iago is using Roderigo and taking money from him.
5   Othello is a great storyteller.
6   Desdemona's love for Othello is true.

Act 2, Scene 1

The action moves to Cyprus where news arrives that a storm has caused the majority of the Turkish fleet to founder, removing the threat. Iago tells Roderigo that Cassio has designs on Desdemona, encouraging him to discredit Cassio and bring about his downfall, which would in turn further Iago's plot to bring about the destruction of Othello.

'News, Lords, your wars are done...'

Act 2 opens with the news that the Turkish fleet has been virtually eliminated by a storm that has been raging around the island. While the danger from the Turks appears to be over, the danger from the elements serves to enhance the dramatic tension of the scene as the whereabouts of the fleet from Venice is called into question. Montano, the outgoing governor of the island, waits expectantly for news regarding his replacement, Othello. Cassio is the first to land safely on the island and reassures the governor that the general will be

Othello

safe. This provides Montano with the opportunity to reflect on the character of Othello, speaking of him in glowing terms and echoing the views of the Duke of Venice when he comments on Othello's capacity as a soldier. Othello, according to Montano, is 'worthy', 'brave' and a 'full soldier'. Iago's view of Othello is now convincingly shown to be a slanderous one.

While the uncertainty of Othello's arrival continues, Montano engages in conversation with Cassio concerning Othello's recent marriage to Desdemona. Cassio is complimentary about Desdemona and states that she is both beautiful and virtuous. Cassio's description of Desdemona is courteous and proper and confirms that he is a refined and courtly man, a point that will ironically be his downfall. As news of Desdemona's arrival filters through, Cassio uses hyperbole to describe her and concedes that he is not surprised that she has arrived safely, as the common natural elements must part for the 'divine Desdemona.' Cassio's courtly description of Desdemona is given added propriety as he continues to urge the arrival of Othello so that he can 'come to Desdemona's arms.' Although Cassio speaks flatteringly of Desdemona, there is no suggestion that he has any thoughts of an improper relationship with her.

Iago

It is interesting to note that Iago's deception of characters is quite universal: here, Cassio refers to Iago as being trustworthy and 'bold', which suggests none of the ill-feeling which Iago harbours for the lieutenant.

When Desdemona enters Cassio is courteous and flattering to his general's wife, who is polite in her reply but whose first thoughts are for her husband and whether Cassio has information of his safety. As news of another ship's arrival, almost certainly Othello's, is received, Desdemona and Iago launch into a strange yet revealing conversation.

Cassio courteously kisses Emilia, Iago's wife, on her arrival, and as the

Iago

company awaits news of Othello, Desdemona and Iago discuss the nature of women. In a superficially roguish and playful way Iago gradually reveals his cynical and negative view of women. Desdemona, in spite of her concerns for the safety of Othello, engages Iago in the conversation and attempts to defend women. Iago sees women as manipulative and demanding, using their sexuality to get their own way and being positively wanton in their pursuit of sex. Desdemona treats Iago's words as if they are a crude joke, but knowing what we do of Iago, how do you view the conversation between the two characters? Does it explain some of Iago's grievances?

As Desdemona looks to Cassio to frown upon Iago's bawdy talk, Iago himself uses their interchange to turn aside and ruminate on his plans. It is clear that Iago sees the opportunity to use Cassio's courtliness to undo him. He is explicit in stating that he will use Cassio's 'own courtesies' to bring suspicion on him. The social status of Cassio is here implicitly attacked: Cassio's constant display of mannerly behaviour is consistent with that shown in the court and upper echelons of society. Iago, who is without these mannerisms, is obviously resentful and he revels in the imminent realisation of his plan to remove Cassio from his 'lieutenantry'. Iago begins to spin a web of deceit, and the image of this web trapping 'as big a fly as Cassio' is disturbing and ominous.

'If it were now to die/'Twere to be most happy...'

The arrival of Othello provides the audience another opportunity to see the

Love

love that exists between the newly married couple. The tone of this public and enthusiastic declaration of love contrasts sharply with that of Iago's private and sinister machinations and serves as a timely reminder of what Iago's plans will ultimately destroy. There is acute irony in Othello's words (above) as he goes on to say that he fears that he is so much in love that his happiness is absolute and he cannot see how it could get any better: these words will come to haunt him.

Desdemona's love is equally great and she feels that their love can only increase as time goes on. The only discord that Othello can see for this love is in the fluctuating beat of their hearts as they kiss, which they proceed to do as another public affirmation of their love. At this point Othello is well satisfied: the Turks have been defeated by nature and his term as governor of Cyprus has begun peacefully; he looks forward to happy times ahead. He accuses himself of 'prattling' and refers constantly to Desdemona as 'honey' and 'sweet'. The dramatic irony of Othello's speech is heightened when he speaks of Iago in glowing terms – the words 'good', 'worthiness' and 'respect' are all used in association with Iago in the space of three lines (207–210).

Examination

Iago positively relishes the thought of bringing about the destruction of Othello and Desdemona. It almost appears that he delights in the thought of bringing disorder to a scene of harmony. See examination question 2, page 69.

Iago and Roderigo are left alone after all the other characters leave, and

Iago

they speak to each other in prose, reflecting the sordid nature of their conversation. The first seed in Iago's plan is sown as he falsely informs Roderigo that Cassio is in love with Desdemona. It is clear from Roderigo's response that, in spite of his infatuation with Desdemona, he cannot believe this after having seen the way that Othello and Desdemona have so openly displayed their love. Iago plays on Roderigo's prejudices suggesting, as he did in Act 1, Scene 3, that the love of Othello and Desdemona is based purely in lust and violent passion which is now spent. Iago implies that Othello can no longer engage the lusty Desdemona with his rough, uncultured charm and that she is now seeking someone who is her social equal.

Desdemona will look for a 'second choice', and who else appears to embody the manners and breeding of a gentleman but Cassio? Iago's description of Cassio beginning 'a knave very voluble' and ending 'a subtle slippery knave, a finder out of occasions; that has an eye can stamp and counterfeit the true advantages never present themselves' (lines 236–242) is almost a direct description of himself, and the irony of this speech should not be lost on the audience.

As well as attacking Cassio, Iago implies that Desdemona is lustful and a willing partner in this alleged deceit. Roderigo interjects again with 'I cannot believe that in her, she's full of most blest condition.' Iago's negative view of women surfaces again as he mocks Roderigo's idealised view and suggests that Desdemona and Cassio have had the gall to publicly 'paddle' hands. Roderigo accurately perceives this as 'courtesy' and remains unconvinced, so Iago continues to press his case, accusing both Cassio and Desdemona of lechery, and reminding Roderigo that he has come to Cyprus under Iago's guidance: 'But sir, be you rul'd by me.' Roderigo's lowly position in society is highlighted here as Iago reveals that while Roderigo has travelled with Othello's entourage he is not known to Cassio. Iago instructs Roderigo to provoke Cassio in some way that will publicly disgrace him. Note that, after everything Iago has said, Roderigo still remains unconvinced, although it could be cowardice rather than conscience that is the determining factor now that Iago has mentioned the possibility of trouble. Ultimately it is Roderigo's 'desire' for Desdemona that sways him into participation in Iago's plan and he leaves believing that if he helps Iago bring about the downfall of Cassio he will have the opportunity to woo Desdemona. Why do you think it takes Iago a relatively long time in dramatic terms to convince Roderigo to help him usurp Cassio? What is the dramatic effect created here?

'that I put the Moor,/At least, into a jealousy so strong...'

Roderigo departs with assurances that he will try to follow Iago's instructions and Othello's ensign is left alone again to soliloquise. Iago's motives for

Jealousy

revenge are more confused now. Initially his main grudge against Othello and Cassio was the fact that he had been overlooked for promotion, however, at this point in the play Iago seems to want to destroy both Cassio and Othello because of sexual jealousy. Iago now implicates Cassio as well as Othello for having sexual relations with his wife, Emilia. There is no evidence, nor will there be, that either of these characters, as Iago states, 'Hath leap'd into my seat'. Iago's motive is very subjective and lacks real substance, but his intent now is to either enjoy Desdemona sexually, 'wife, for wife' or, failing that, to instil in Othello a 'jealousy so strong,/That judgement cannot cure' so that his happiness will be ruined.

Iago's view of different characters is revealed here: he considers Roderigo 'poor trash of Venice', yet, more interestingly, he acknowledges begrudgingly that Othello has 'a constant, noble, loving nature'. However, Iago intends to use these traits of Othello's to bring about his destruction.

Examination

There is clear evidence that the Iago's plotting is fairly immediate and spontaneous. He is thinking aloud here and his plan emerges from his conjecture. Iago is to 'abuse' Cassio to Othello after Roderigo has caused trouble with him and is then to receive Othello's thanks for being a loyal servant to him. Iago's plan is still in its infancy and has yet to take on its full shape, even in his own mind, as the last two lines of the scene reveal: ''tis here, but yet confused;/Knavery's plain face is never seen, till us'd.' See examination question 2, page 69.

Act 2, Scene 2

Othello invites the people of Cyprus to celebrate his marriage to Desdemona and the thwarting of the Turkish threat.

'Heaven bless the isle of Cyprus, and our noble general Othello!'

This short scene is used primarily to show the passage of time, driving the plot forward by a number of hours. However, there appears to be a layer of dramatic irony in the proclamation. Othello wishes to provide everyone on the island with the opportunity to celebrate and to encourage 'each man to what sport and revels his mind leads him.' While most of the islanders and guests will join in the celebrations, Iago will use them to initiate his plot. Othello's magnanimity and keenness for others to enjoy the happiness he feels will be the beginning of his destruction.

Act 2, Scene 3

Iago persuades Cassio, who is on watch, to drink, knowing that he is not a drinker and that he will be easy to antagonise. Roderigo provokes Cassio into a fight and Othello, hearing the disturbance, arrives to find the nobleman Montano seriously injured.

'I have very poor and unhappy brains for drinking.'

The opening of this scene presents us with a brief interchange between Cassio and Othello in which, once again, Iago's 'honesty' is mentioned. Cassio assures the general that he will personally oversee the festivities while Othello and Desdemona retire.

As the newlyweds exit to consummate their marriage, Cassio is joined on the watch by Iago. It is interesting to note that Iago immediately begins to speak in prose, indicating the tone he is to adopt throughout the scene. He remarks that it is still early and that Othello has only retired so that he can enjoy a night of passion with his new bride. Iago embarks upon a fairly

Desdemona

personal and arguably crude analysis of Desdemona. In the dialogue that ensues, notice how all of Cassio's remarks are polite, courteous and complimentary to Desdemona; Iago, on the other hand, is fairly explicit. Contrast the use of language: Iago suggests that Desdemona is wanton, that she is 'full of game' and 'sport' and that there is 'provocation' in her eye; Cassio states that she is 'exquisite', 'fresh', 'delicate', 'modest' and 'perfection'. Crudity here clashes with idealism. Why do you think this conversation takes place? What does this scene tell us about each character's view of women?

Iago encourages Cassio to drink a 'stoup of wine'. Cassio, by his own admission, is not a drinker and is easily made drunk. However, Iago convinces

Iago

Cassio that it is in honour of Othello that he should integrate himself into the festivities, so Cassio reluctantly agrees. As Cassio leaves to call in some revelling companions, Iago has the opportunity to consider his plans in a soliloquy, revealing his intention to ply Cassio with drink so that he loses control and becomes quarrelsome, ensuring that he will get into a fight when he encounters Roderigo. Cassio, who has been left in a position of responsibility by Othello, will shame himself and his office.

Iago's treachery is demonstrated further after Cassio leaves for the watch,

Appearance

clearly drunk but protesting his sobriety. Iago, when speaking with Montano, the outgoing governor of Cyprus and clearly an important, influential and powerful man, skilfully calls into question Cassio's integrity. Iago manages here, as he does on numerous occasions, to suggest support and concern for an individual while systematically destroying their credibility. He mentions to Montano that Cassio is a 'soldier fit to stand by Caesar', but that his vice (drinking) sadly matches his virtue, and implies that he drinks every night. Iago's apparent concern spreads further as he implicitly criticises Othello's judgement for trusting Cassio to be his deputy. Montano is concerned and suggests that Othello be made aware of the situation. While Montano continues to suggest that Iago should inform the general of the matter, Roderigo appears and is surreptitiously dispatched by Iago to follow Cassio and cause an affray. Iago protests to Montano that he is reluctant to highlight Cassio's problems to Othello as he 'loves' Cassio and would not wish to do him harm. The irony of the situation is heightened by the fact that once Montano suggests it would be an 'honest action' to inform Othello, Iago declines.

'Cassio I love thee,/But never more be officer of mine.'

Iago's plan works to perfection, with Cassio reappearing enraged and angling for a fight with Roderigo. Cassio loses control and strikes Roderigo; Montano tries to intercede and is pulled into the squabble as well, eventually exchanging blows with Cassio. Roderigo, again under direction from Iago, raises the alarm. Notice the dramatic irony of Iago's actions here (line 149) as he pretends to be the peacemaker, and later (lines 158–159) when Othello enters

to restore peace and Iago reiterates his plea for a sense of duty and place. In Othello's speech, beginning at line 160, we see a glimpse of the anger that is to be so manipulated and fuelled by Iago later in the play. Othello, here, is a man of action – gone are the soft words of love and in come the direct and brutal commands of a successful general. He reasserts his

Othello

Christianity and reminds the trouble makers that it is the Turks who are the common enemy. It could be argued that even at this moment Othello feels the need to clearly define himself as being an accepted part of Venetian society, another weakness that Iago will exploit later.

Ironically it is to 'honest Iago' that Othello now turns and asks for an

explanation. Iago's performance is exemplary. Without being disloyal to Othello or to Cassio he says that he is oblivious as to the cause of the fight. Cassio refuses to speak, which later proves to be to Iago's advantage, and Montano is too injured to speak. Othello demands an explanation from Iago and,

Appearance

ironically, Montano calls upon Iago's honour as a soldier to tell the truth. Playing the part of a dutiful servant but also friend to Cassio, Iago seemingly reluctantly recounts his version of the night's events. His account seals the fate of Cassio. While trying to save Cassio by making excuses for him, Iago ensures that Othello will have no other option than to remove him from office for causing such a shameful public display.

Look closely at the way Iago, using his supplications for Cassio, raises his own standing. The irony of Iago's dramatic and fiercely ironic opening line underpins his whole account. We know that Cassio has no chance of escaping the wrath of Othello when Iago states 'I had rather ha' this tongue cut from my mouth,/Than it should do offence to Michael Cassio.' Iago constantly tries to underplay Cassio's part in the fight, but with subtle additions such as, 'And Cassio high in oaths, which till tonight/I ne'er might see before' and, 'But men are men, the best sometimes forget,' gradually reveals that Cassio has, in fact, acted in a disgraceful manner not befitting such a high-ranking officer. Othello's response to Iago's story shows that the only character who has managed to come through the scenario with any credit is Iago himself! Othello's reaction is concise and obviously difficult for him: 'Cassio, I love thee,/But never more be officer of mine.'

Cassio is left in shame and is consoled by Iago. Cassio's chief concern is that he has lost his good name and reputation, without which he considers himself to have lost the distinction that separates man from beast. He is extremely hard on himself and ashamed of his behaviour. Iago begins, once

again, to manipulate Cassio's goodwill, suggesting that Othello will forgive him, convincing him that his actions have not done irreparable damage and that his former position is re-attainable. Iago cleverly suggests that the way to convince Othello that this has been an isolated error of judgement on Cassio's part is through Othello's 'general', Desdemona. The

Iago

qualities that Cassio himself has already identified in Desdemona are the surest way to appease Othello's anger. Desdemona is the key to restoring Cassio to his position. Iago encourages Cassio to ask Desdemona to plead his case to Othello, advice that is readily accepted by Cassio as he sees this as a way back into Othello's favour. This time it is Cassio who is fooled by Iago's false loyalty, echoing Othello's earlier praise by referring to Iago as 'honest'.

'I play the villain?'

Iago is again left alone to consider his actions and assess the progress of his

machinations. He has achieved the discrediting of Cassio, but another avenue has opened up for Iago. As Cassio, in shame, has refused to attempt to justify his actions to Othello, Iago senses that this could work to his advantage, providing the opportunity for the destruction of Othello and Desdemona.

Revenge

Examination

Iago's plotting, which has been superbly improvised up to this point, now takes on a coherent shape – he is clear in his determination to 'enmesh 'em all.' He seems to be treating their destruction as some kind of intellectual challenge and is wallowing in his own superiority. See examination question 2, page 69.

Roderigo enters again as a pitiful figure, providing some light relief, if only momentarily, from Iago's disturbing soliloquy. Iago persuades Roderigo to have patience and implies that now Cassio is no longer an obstacle Desdemona will soon be his. Gullible as ever, Roderigo exits and we are given the next stage of Iago's plan. His language is more concise and he sets down clear objectives for the success of his plan. He will persuade his wife to encourage Desdemona to take up Cassio's cause, then he will ensure that Othello sees the secret meeting that will take place. The final line of the act is both definite and chilling as Iago determines to act without delay to realise his villainy. How do you view Iago's plotting? Do you think Iago reacts to opportunities or has the destruction of Othello been his main intention throughout? Does Iago's speech at the end of Act 2 differ from his earlier soliloquies?

■ Self-test questions Act 2

Who? What? Why? When? Where? How?
1   Whose ship is the first to arrive in Cyprus?
2   What is Cassio's 'bold show of courtesy' to Desdemona?
3   Why does Othello order celebrations on the island of Cyprus?
4   When does the watch begin?
5   Where does Iago send Roderigo and for what reason?
6   How does Iago convince Cassio to continue drinking?
7   Who encourages Cassio to ask Desdemona for help and why?
8   What reason does Iago give to Roderigo to convince him to provoke Cassio?
9   Why doesn't Montano provide Othello with the details of the street brawl?
10 How does Iago intend to use Emilia in his plotting?

Who said this, and why?
1   'Reputation, reputation, I ha' lost my reputation...'
2   'If it were now to die,/'Twere now to be most happy.'
3   'as little a web as this will ensnare as great a fly as Cassio.'
4   'Cassio I love thee,/But never more be officer of mine.'
5   'And out of her goodness make the net/That shall enmesh 'em all.'

Prove it!
Provide comment and textual evidence to prove the following statements.
1   Iago intends to use his wife Emilia to help him with his plans.
2   The Turkish fleet is destroyed by the stormy weather.
3   Cassio shows courtesy to Desdemona.
4   Iago speaks crudely about women.
5   Othello is convinced that he and Desdemona are going to be happy on Cyprus.

Act 3, Scene 1

Emilia agrees to set up a private meeting between Cassio and Desdemona.

Cassio and a clown

Some much needed comic relief is provided at the beginning of this act by the clown. Following Venetian tradition Cassio has paid for musicians to play to celebrate Othello's wedding night. Unfortunately the music has not pleased the general and he dispatches the clown to pay the musicians to stop. The clown's bawdy comments to the musicians are soon overshadowed by his dramatic purpose: the clown has access to Emilia and Cassio pays him to deliver a message to her to meet with him immediately. The entrance of Iago gives added expediency to Cassio's request and he is soon provided with the opportunity to set up a meeting with Desdemona, through Emilia. Cassio's final words reveal how much he is at the mercy of Iago as he suggests to Emilia 'I am bound to thee forever.'

Act 3, Scene 2

A brief scene in which we see the general carrying out his military duties as governor.

The purpose of this scene appears to be twofold. Firstly, we see Othello clearly in control of his military duties and, secondly, we see his increasing reliance on Iago now that he is without a lieutenant.

Act 3, Scene 3

Desdemona agrees to appeal to Othello on Cassio's behalf. Iago plants suspicion in Othello's mind about Desdemona's fidelity. Othello begins to talk of murderous vengeance, and gives Iago three days to kill Cassio. Iago is promoted to lieutenant and pledges his loyalty to Othello.

Major developments

This is the pivotal scene in the play, as it is the one where Iago convinces

Revenge

Othello that both his wife and best friend have committed adultery. Othello, at the end of the scene, determines to take his revenge by murdering them both. Iago's planning and manipulation will determine, from this point onwards, the tragic outcome of the play in an inevitable and unstoppable chain of events.

Desdemona

It is significant, therefore, that the scene opens with a conversation between Desdemona and Cassio which shows that the feelings the two characters have for each other are based purely on respect, and their relationship is defined through their common love for Othello. The cheerful optimism shown by Desdemona is soon to be overshadowed by Iago's machinations. Cassio is desperate to return to Othello's 'love and service' and he feels that this needs to happen quickly. Desdemona vows to pursue Cassio's cause relentlessly, as Iago knew she would.

Coursework

Desdemona's premise for helping Cassio is, in a sense, to restore equilibrium to Othello's mind. She acknowledges their friendship: 'you do love my lord,/You have known him long'. This is consistent with Desdemona's good-natured disposition and her love for Othello. The development of her character is far from contrived (see the coursework question on page 64).

Cassio departs as he sees Othello and Iago approach, because he is still too ashamed to face Othello. Cassio's reticence again provides Iago with the opportunity to implement the process that will ultimately result in the downfall of the central characters. As Cassio leaves Iago suggests that his motives for talking to Desdemona have been less than innocent: 'Ha, I like not that', and 'Cassio my lord? ... No, I cannot think it,/That he would sneak away so guilty-like,/Seeing you coming.' Notice the way that Othello's doubt is immediately shown through the language that he uses. Gone is the assertive general and the eloquent lover as his speech is riddled with short questions which are left, for most part, unanswered.

Iago

The openness shown by Desdemona should alleviate any fears that Othello has, but his insecurity, which is cleverly manipulated by Iago, is evident. Desdemona begins to push relentlessly for Othello to reconsider his actions with regard to Cassio. She appeals to Othello's power and grace as a great leader to reconsider his decision and forgive Cassio.

'Whate'er you be, I am obedient...'

Othello, it appears, can deny Desdemona nothing and he eventually agrees to consider the position of Cassio. Desdemona reminds Othello that Cassio has been an integral part in her wooing, carrying love tokens and messages between the two lovers, but Iago will later subvert this thought to further imply improper behaviour between the general's wife and best friend. Othello's love for Desdemona is made explicit when he reasserts the importance of his wife's love after she has left. Othello says that if he lost Desdemona's love then chaos would ensue. The irony of Othello's words is to resonate through the rest of the scene. It is clear that Iago's words have had a direct impact upon him; he wants to grant Desdemona's wishes, yet he has to ask her to give him time alone. Dutiful as ever, the loyal and faithful Desdemona does as she is requested. As she exits her words are heavy with irony, 'be it as your fancies teach you...', and we see throughout the rest of the scene how Othello's fancies will ultimately lead to Desdemona's death.

Love

The interchange between Iago and Othello that follows Desdemona's exit is dramatically stunning. Iago continues to manipulate Othello through his use of implication and insinuation. Notice how Iago raises doubts in Othello by, for most part, repeating the questions that Othello throws at him. Iago does not directly assert any allegations, instead he increases Othello's exasperation by saying nothing but implying much. Iago questions Cassio's honesty, and he uses the fact that Cassio has had access to Desdemona on behalf of Othello to imply that their liaisons have been less

Iago

than innocent. Eventually Iago's echoing of Othello's questions inflames Othello's temper, which increases in its intensity throughout the rest of this scene. Iago, both in linguistic and actual terms, is in the position of power at this moment. Othello's doubts and fears about his wife's fidelity, and his insecurities regarding his standing in Venetian society are all mercilessly exploited by Iago.

Iago knows that he must convince Othello of his wife's infidelity through suggestion before he actually puts it into words. Othello repeatedly asks Iago to reveal his thoughts – by delaying this Iago increases the tension and the exasperation felt by Othello.

Appearance

Iago is only able to make these insinuations because Othello considers him an 'honest' man who is loyal to him and who loves him. Othello believes that Iago is measuring his words and refusing to speak because he realises the enormity of what he has to say. It is ironic that Othello is sure that if Iago were a 'false, disloyal knave' his delays and hesitations would be 'tricks of custom', which unfortunately they are! Iago uses Othello's perception of him to call into question Cassio's honesty. Iago 'thinks' that Cassio is honest as he 'seems' to be so. Iago cleverly manipulates Othello into pursuing the matter and the general asks him to reveal his innermost thoughts concerning Cassio. Once again Iago delays, heightening the dramatic tension and giving the impression that he does not want to upset Othello by voicing his concerns. It is clearly Iago who is in control of the situation – Othello's responses are reduced to exclamations between lines 148 and 200 as Iago implies that Othello must control his jealousy or risk losing his good name.

'This fellow's of exceeding honesty...'

Iago has cleverly manipulated Othello into feeling confused and uneasy. Remember that many of the other characters in the play have commented on Iago's honesty and trustworthiness: Othello has no reason to think that Iago would lie to him. Indeed, Iago has previously spoken up for Cassio (Act 2, Scene 3, line 132) by suggesting that anyone can be susceptible to errors of judgement. Of course, the audience realises that in fact Iago is condemning Cassio by highlighting the serious nature of the error. Othello's uneasiness is

Jealousy

now transformed by Iago into a specific emotion – jealousy. Iago's warnings to guard against the 'green-ey'd monster' are met with scorn by Othello. He suggests that he would not waste his life feeling insecure and suspicious, but that once an infidelity had been uncovered he would be 'resolved' and unforgiving. These ominous words are tempered somewhat by his faith in Desdemona; he realises that she is 'fair' and attractive, but his insecurities are appeased by the fact that Desdemona chose him. He would require proof to believe any suggestions of infidelity, and if he had proof his response would be deadly.

Iago, once again, seizes his opportunity. Othello's words ultimately give Iago licence to utter his false suspicions about an illicit affair between Cassio and Desdemona. Look at the contrast between the speech of the two characters at this point: Othello's speech (lines 180–196) is verbose and full of grandeur, whereas Iago's (lines 197–208) is brief and succinct. Gone is the meandering and implicit suggestion of earlier speeches in the scene as Iago, sensing that Othello is susceptible to doubt, at last reveals his 'fears'. Iago suggests to Othello that he is only making these accusations out of duty and

Iago

love to the general, and his earlier hesitancy has implied that what he has to say must have an element of truth in it. Iago's skilful delaying tactics have prepared the ground for these false accusations and, sensing that Othello is vulnerable, Iago speaks 'with franker spirit' and eventually shifts from vague generalisations to specific revelations. To protect his position Iago says that he has only suspicions and no firm proof, but he advises Othello to observe Desdemona's behaviour when she is with Cassio.

To reinforce his accusations Iago targets Othello's weaknesses – he knows

Othello

that Othello is not comfortable with his social position in Venetian society, that he is insecure in the manners and customs of the court and that he constantly seeks reassurance that he is, indeed, worthy to be part of such society. Iago implies that that Desdemona's disloyalty is a common feature of Venetian society and Othello, inexperienced in these

matters, is inclined to accept Iago's word. Iago also reminds Othello that Desdemona has broken a bond before with ease – that with her own father – and so is likely to do the same again with her husband. Iago compounds Othello's doubts and suspicions while, at the same time, ensuring that he will not directly challenge Desdemona's infidelity for fear of humiliating himself socially: if Othello challenges Desdemona she may well pour scorn on Othello's social naïvety by suggesting that this is common practice in Venice.

Love

Iago returns constantly to the fact that he is only revealing his innermost fears because he 'loves' Othello and he is 'bound' to him in terms of honour and duty. He even suggests that his fears may be exaggerated because he loves the general too much and is overly concerned with protecting his position. In terms of dramatic irony Iago's villainy is fascinating.

Appearance

Iago returns here, as he does on other occasions, to the idea of appearance. Desdemona has fooled her own father to such an extent that he believed she had been a victim of witchcraft when he found out she had married Othello. Iago therefore implies that it would be easy for Desdemona to dupe Othello.

Othello is now completely under the spell of Iago. The idea of bonding is repeated as Othello echoes Iago's words, 'I am bound to thee for ever' – there is a sense that Othello's fate is tragically sealed. The effect of Iago's words on Othello is apparent in his diminished speech: it is undermined by negatives (lines 218, 225, 228 and 229) and the emotional and mental strain on Othello is obvious as he begins to drift into an open monologue with himself about the honesty of his wife. Othello is now so affected by Iago's suggestions that he wishes to be left on his own. As Iago leaves we see the full impact of the revelations on Othello: he requests that Iago report back any further findings and he asks him to set his wife, Emilia, to spy on Desdemona.

Othello is so convinced of Iago's loyalty that he thinks his ensign is holding back information purely to protect him. Iago returns and interrupts Othello's thoughts by trying to play down the suggestions that he has made, claiming that he is probably wrong. However, knowing that Cassio, under his direction, is to privately appeal to Desdemona to support him in his reinstatement, Iago warns Othello to watch out for Desdemona supporting Cassio's cause as 'Much will be seen in that', and it will be further proof that the relationship between the two characters is less than innocent. Iago, just before he leaves, repeats that his fears are most probably unfounded: his attempts to play down his accusations are skilfully engineered to heighten Othello's fears.

'If she be false, O, then heaven mocks itself,/I'll not believe it.'

Othello's soliloquy shows how far the words of Iago have penetrated. Othello is shown, through his use of language, to be riddled with doubt and insecurity: he laments his lack of social graces, and blames his race and even his age for causing Desdemona to be unfaithful to him. It is obvious that Othello has begun to convince himself of Desdemona's infidelity even before he has proof. It is only when Desdemona approaches that Othello seems momentarily to break free of the spell of doubt, declaring that he will not believe in Desdemona's infidelity. It is interesting and foreboding that such is the strength of Othello's feelings that if Desdemona has been unfaithful he will lose his faith in heaven ('heaven mocks itself...'), echoing his words of earlier in the scene.

Chance now plays a crucial role in the play as Iago manages to obtain the means to provide Othello with some circumstantial yet, in his present state of mind, convincing evidence of Desdemona's unfaithfulness. The evidence is a handkerchief, a love token given by Othello to Desdemona to first express his love for her. Desdemona enters, ever the dutiful wife, to remind Othello that his presence is expected at a civil dinner. Othello admits he has been preoccupied and has therefore forgotten. Desdemona immediately spots that there is something wrong with Othello and, thinking that he has a headache, she attempts to soothe his brow with her handkerchief. The 'napkin' is too small and is inadvertently dropped on the floor. With Othello distracted and Desdemona concerned the handkerchief is forgotten and both characters exit.

Emilia's intentions here are ambiguous: she realises the handkerchief has great sentimental value for Desdemona, but she opts to pass it on to her husband who 'hath a hundred times' asked her to steal it. Emilia is obviously torn about what to do, but she resolves to 'ha' the work ta'en out' and pass it on to her husband. Iago enters and his first action is to 'chide' Emilia and question her as to why she is alone, and when she tells him that she has something for him he responds with an insult by calling her 'foolish' – Iago obviously does not treat Emilia well, and it is understandable that she is keen to placate him by complying with his wishes. We again see Iago's negative view of women – his demeanour to Emilia softens when he realises that she has Desdemona's handkerchief, but he still manages affectionately to call her a wench and ultimately snatches the handkerchief from her when she questions him concerning its use. Emilia seems to have a subservient fear of Iago, and she leaves the stage obediently even though she knows that Desdemona will be upset at the loss of the token.

Coursework

Emilia, in spite of her feelings for Desdemona, obviously wishes to please her husband. Her motive for passing the handkerchief to Iago appears to be simply to gain his favour. Do you feel sympathy for Emilia, or is this just evidence of dramatic contrivance? See the coursework question on page 64.

Jealousy

Iago's soliloquy that follows reveals his intent to use the handkerchief as 'proof' that Desdemona and Cassio are engaged in an illicit affair. Iago knows now that he can fully manipulate Othello's jealousy and insecurity by making 'trifles light as air [appear] as proofs of holy writ...'. By placing the handkerchief in Cassio's lodgings circumstantial evidence will become hard proof to the vulnerable Othello. Iago positively basks in his success at manipulating Othello's emotions and readily admits that his 'poison' is already working on the rationality of the general. Iago knows that Othello will never sleep soundly again and takes a villainous satisfaction in the result of his actions as Othello appears in a state of obvious distress, talking to himself about Desdemona.

'Avaunt, be gone, thou hast set me on the rack...'
Othello is almost out of his mind at this point and he lashes out at Iago for being the one who has told him about Desdemona's infidelity. It is clear, now,

Jealousy

that Othello has fallen for Iago's lies: he fully accepts that Desdemona has slept with Cassio in 'stol'n hours of lust...'. While he did not know of his wife's indiscretion it did not hurt him, but now that he does know he feels that he has been robbed of his equanimity and that he can no longer function in his role as a soldier – he seems to have lost his sense of self.

It appears that here, possibly for the first time in the play, Iago has miscalculated and loses control of the situation. His intention to awaken a violent jealousy in Othello has clearly worked, but at this point in the play much of Othello's anger is directed at Iago. In his rage Othello calls Iago a 'villain' and threatens that if his accusations prove slanderous he will pay dearly. Othello asks for 'ocular proof' before he will believe his wife's wrongdoing.

Revenge

This is a critical moment in the play, full of dramatic tension: Othello touches upon the truth ('If thou dost slander her, and torture me,') and threatens Iago again with death. Othello's anger is almost uncontrollable; it is similar to that of King Lear as he threatens to make his retribution unearthly.

Iago's speech is reduced to a series of short statements and rhetorical questions as Othello rages. Iago, at this crucial stage of the play, responds with indignation. His exclamations are forceful and he repents that he has been honest only to be repaid with mistrust and threats – the irony is rich, yet his outburst (lines 379–386) appears to curb Othello's anger, and once again Iago regains the initiative.

Look at the crudity of Iago's speech from lines 400 to 415. The graphic

Iago

references to sexual intercourse are effective in debilitating Othello. Iago builds up a visual picture of Desdemona's infidelity which he will later solidify with reference to the handkerchief. With Othello in a deeply distressed and vulnerable state Iago offers further incriminating evidence by suggesting that he has heard Cassio call out Desdemona's name and utter terms of endearment in his sleep. Othello unquestioningly believes Iago, who again plays down the importance of his words and urges caution from Othello, 'Nay, this was but his dream.' For Othello, suggestion has now become fact and, as Iago says, this will 'help to thicken other proofs'. Othello now resolves to kill Desdemona, 'I'll tear her all to pieces', and Iago realises that this is now inevitable regardless of what his intentions had been initially.

With Othello in the palm of his hand Iago refers to the handkerchief that he has in his possession, which Desdemona dropped earlier in the scene. He says that the handkerchief is now in Cassio's possession in spite of its sentimental significance to Desdemona. Iago's intention to convince Othello of betrayal is now complete. Othello's use of language changes as he speaks of 'black vengeance', hatred, revenge and, most chillingly, 'blood'. Othello's 'bloody thoughts' are now as inevitable and unstoppable as an ebbing sea as he uses a natural image to justify what will be his unnatural behaviour.

Revenge

Othello is now on his knees, where he is joined by Iago as the two characters swear a dark and bloody pact of revenge. Iago appears to pledge his undying and absolute loyalty by accepting that in order to avenge 'wrong'd Othello' he will perform 'what bloody work so ever'. Othello asks Iago to bring about the death of Cassio and says that he will dispose of Desdemona. Iago's triumph seems complete as Othello promotes his ensign to the rank of lieutenant. The scene ends with Iago dutifully pledging his loyalty for ever.

Act 3, Scene 3 shows Iago at the height of his persuasive powers. He manages skilfully and credibly to convince Othello, by suggestion and inference, that Desdemona has been unfaithful (see examination question 2, page 69).

Examination

Act 3, Scene 4

Desdemona pleads Cassio's cause with Othello. He asks to see the love token he has given to her (the handkerchief), which she cannot provide. Cassio enters and is prompted by Iago to speak with Desdemona. Desdemona leaves promising Cassio that she will speak for him again. Cassio gives the handkerchief to his mistress, Bianca, and asks her to copy the embroidery as he likes it.

The handkerchief

The dramatic tension that has built up in the previous scene is relieved for a short time by the opening of this scene, which sees Desdemona requesting that the clown fetch Cassio to her. The clown plays on the word 'lie', and even in this exchange the underlying theme of misconception and falsehood is made apparent. Through the clown's unwillingness to speak plainly a simple task is made difficult. Once the clown has gone in search of Cassio our attention turns once again to the handkerchief. Desdemona is clearly in

Desdemona

distress at misplacing her handkerchief and suggests that if Othello was a naturally jealous man he might suspect her love was not as deep as it is. Emilia's role is crucial here as she remains silent even though she does know the whereabouts of the token: her fear of Iago is greater than her duty towards Desdemona, ultimately adding to the tragic outcome of the play. The dramatic irony is clear: just as Desdemona is discussing Othello's incapacity to be jealous the envy-ridden general enters.

The strain on Othello is obvious. On first seeing Desdemona he addresses her formally as 'my good lady' and he admits, in an aside, that he is finding it hard to pretend ('dissemble') that nothing is wrong. Even though Othello strives to remain in control, his conversation with Desdemona is littered with implicit references to loyalty and infidelity. As soon as Desdemona speaks for Cassio, however, the physical effect on Othello is evident. He uses this as an opportunity to request the use of Desdemona's handkerchief.

Othello's storytelling skills come to the fore again when Desdemona cannot give him the handkerchief, which now takes on a symbolic significance. Othello weaves a tale about the love token being charmed and, therefore, representative of fidelity and devotion: if the handkerchief is lost, the spell of love will be broken. Desdemona, of course, is well aware that she has misplaced the handkerchief and her turmoil and distress are clear. Othello is relentless in his demand to see the handkerchief and, in desperation, Desdemona tries to change the subject by pursuing the case of Cassio. This, of course, enrages Othello further and his speech, which has already been broken and erratic, is reduced to a single demand: 'The handkerchief!' Ironically, Desdemona punctuates his demand with further pleas for Cassio which ultimately result in Othello storming off.

'Heaven keep that monster from Othello's mind!'

The theme of jealousy is presented through Othello's actions and through Emilia's reaction to the scene, 'Is not this man jealous?' Desdemona's reaction is one of disbelief as she laments the loss of the handkerchief. Emilia's cynicism is displayed here: she knows where the handkerchief is, yet she uses the situation to make a generalised comment about the nature of men, echoing the misogyny of her husband.

Cassio enters and beseeches Desdemona to use her influence to restore him to Othello's favour. Desdemona intimates that there is a problem with Othello and that he does not appear to be himself, and she tries to console herself that Othello's mood has been caused by some affairs of state. Her idealised opinion of her husband is forced into reality when she acknowledges that 'Men are not gods...', and that Othello is in a responsible position that brings with it many pressures. Emilia suggests that it may not be public matters but private matters that are disturbing Othello, and she ominously suggests that he may be jealous. In response to Desdemona's direct and innocent 'I never gave him cause!', Emilia once again echoes Iago's words as she personifies jealousy as a monster born without cause. These words resonate through the play.

This is the first time we have seen Cassio's mistress, Bianca, and her introduction seems to reflect some of the major themes in the play – love and jealousy – as well as giving us an alternative view of Cassio. His behaviour with women shows him to be a charmer, and his relationship with Bianca, who is viewed by some as a prostitute, is an added complication. Cassio is not meant to be a perfect human being and Shakespeare adds dimension to his character at this point. In spite of this relationship, Cassio's innocence in his dealings with Desdemona is clear to the audience, and he treats Bianca with respect, referring to her as 'sweet' and 'fair' on a number of occasions. He

Jealousy

only becomes annoyed when Bianca presumes the handkerchief he shows her is from another woman. He condemns Bianca for her jealousy and shows that he is honest in his relationship with her. He gives her the handkerchief so that she can copy it as he finds the embroidery pleasing. However, he wishes her to leave before Othello returns: his position is more important to him than his relationship with Bianca, but he is at pains to tell her that he will visit her and she leaves reluctantly. Do you think Bianca's introduction raises questions about Cassio's honesty, or is Shakespeare attempting to reveal to the audience that Cassio is a three-dimensional character?

■ Self-test questions Act 3

Who? What? Why? When? Where? How?
1   Who finds the handkerchief?
2   What message does Cassio send with the clown?
3   Why is Bianca annoyed with Cassio?
4   When does Iago begin to persuade Othello of Desdemona's infidelity?
5   Where does Iago plant the handkerchief?
6   How long does Othello give Iago to murder Cassio?
7   Who does Othello say has given the handkerchief to him?
8   What 'monstrous' image does Iago use to describe jealousy?
9   Why, according to Iago, is it unusual for Othello to be angry?
10 When did Othello give Desdemona the handkerchief?

Who said this, and why?
1   'Be thou assur'd, good Cassio, I will do/All my abilities in thy behalf.'
2   'Ha, I like not that.'
3   'I am bound to thee forever.'
4   'I am glad I have found this napkin..'
5   'you are jealous now/That this is from some mistress, some remembrance.'

Prove it!
Provide comment and textual evidence to prove the following statements.
1   Desdemona is committed to helping Cassio.
2   Othello trusts Iago.
3   Iago is unkind to Emilia.
4   Othello is prepared to murder.
5   The clown is used to relieve the tension.

Act 4, Scene 1

Iago convinces Othello that Cassio and Desdemona are definitely having an affair, and Othello is determined to kill both of them. Iago accepts responsibility for disposing of Cassio and suggests that Othello should strangle Desdemona in her bed. An ambassador from Venice, Lodovico, arrives with a letter ordering Othello's return home. Cassio is to take over the governorship, and Desdemona comments on his worthiness for the post. At this Othello publicly loses his temper and in his fury strikes Desdemona.

'Work on,/My medicine, work...'

The act begins mid-way through a conversation, just as the play opened,

Iago

but this time Iago is fooling Othello rather than Roderigo. Iago suggests that he has found out that Desdemona and Cassio have been 'naked abed together', but that this does not necessarily mean they have been unfaithful! Using the handkerchief as confirmation of infidelity, Iago says that Cassio has admitted to sleeping with Desdemona. Iago's pun on the word 'lie' is cruel yet strikes home. Unable to deal with the mounting evidence, and finally succumbing to Iago's plot, Othello collapses into a stupor. His breakdown is symbolised by his linguistic collapse – his speech is reduced to chaotic prose. Iago is at the height of his powers and has managed to completely dupe Othello; it is hard to find a match for his unrestrained villainy as he gloats over the prostrate body of Othello.

Once Othello has recovered he witnesses a conversation between Iago and

Appearance

Cassio and thinks that they are talking about Desdemona, when in fact they are talking about Bianca. Iago knows that this is what Othello will be thinking, and as he questions Cassio about his relationship with Bianca Othello is driven into a frenzy, as Iago had anticipated. Some critics feel that this is Othello's lowest point yet in the play. While he is being fooled by Iago we feel a semblance of pity for Othello, but now he becomes no more than an eavesdropper who farcically attempts to decode a conversation that is out of earshot. Do you feel that this is Othello's lowest point so far? Does Othello's character plummet even further later on in this scene?

Iago's skilful manipulation of characters continues as he uses Cassio's nonchalant feelings for Bianca to further anger Othello, who thinks that Cassio is discussing his affair with Desdemona. Othello is enraged that Cassio appears to hold such a carefree view of his indiscretion. We are given an insight

Love

into Cassio's character here as he mocks the love Bianca has for him and suggests that he would never marry her, particularly while he is a 'customer', intimating that Iago's previous declaration that Bianca is a prostitute holds some validity: 'A housewife that by selling her desires/Buys herself bread and clothes...'. Cassio is not perfect and his treatment of Bianca seems cruel although, while appearing unsavoury to a modern audience, in its historical context a relationship of this sort would not have been uncommon and merely confirms that Cassio is a human character, not just a dramatic device employed by Shakespeare as a means to bring about Othello's downfall.

'How shall I murder him, Iago?'

Iago's manipulation of Othello is at its height here. Look at the conversation

Iago
between Othello and Iago after Cassio has left the stage. Othello's speech once again breaks down into prose as he resigns himself to the murder of Cassio and Desdemona. Notice the way Iago determines the direction of Othello's thoughts: he mentions the 'ocular proof' of the handkerchief and the fact that Cassio has taken this from Desdemona and has given it, in Iago's words, to his 'whore'. Othello considers Cassio to be the main party to the adultery and begins to comment on Desdemona's virtues, 'a fine woman,/A fair woman, a sweet woman.' However, Iago quickly brings Othello to his senses and attempts to draw him away from positive thoughts. As Othello expounds upon Desdemona's seeming virtues Iago turns this around to make the sin she has apparently committed even greater. Othello is arguably now at his lowest point and completely in the power of Iago. Compare the way Othello is presented to us now with the general who commanded respect in Act 1, Scene 1. How much has he

Revenge
changed? Othello is now determined to kill Desdemona and asks Iago to purchase some poison for him to carry out the deed. It is interesting that Iago suggests an alternative method of killing which is more vicious but protects his position: if Iago buys poison he will be directly linked to Othello's action and his plan will fail. Even at a time like this Iago is alert enough to consider protecting his own position – his sense of self-preservation is exemplary. The fatal conversation ends with Iago promising to take the murder of Cassio in hand.

Just as Othello commits himself to a most corrupt and immoral act Lodovico, a senator from Venice, enters to remind us of Othello's public responsibilities. Othello's descent is now seen through his inability to separate his private feelings from his public duties. As Lodovico asks about Cassio, Desdemona, still intent to honour her promise, speaks about the 'unkind

Othello
breach' which has come about between her husband and his former lieutenant. Innocently and in public Desdemona politely says that she wishes the dispute could be remedied as she 'loves' (in this case, has fond feelings for) Cassio. Othello, in his present state of mind, completely misinterprets this innocent statement and loses control. At first he ignores

Desdemona, then, in response to her words regarding Cassio, he strikes her. The act is, without question, abominable, yet the reaction of the different characters is arguably more significant. The innocence of Desdemona is never more clear as she states plainly 'I have not deserv'd this', and the shocked condemnation of Othello's actions is made explicit by Lodovico's exclamation 'My Lord, this would not be believ'd in Venice...'. Othello is no longer concerned by his public appearance: his jealousy has stripped away all his civility and he has degenerated into an uncultured brute. Ironically, the prejudiced view of Othello voiced earlier by Brabantio, and about which Othello is insecure, now seems to be realised.

Examination

'Is this the noble Moor, whom our full senate/Call all in all sufficient?' (5.1, line 260). This is further proof of Othello's 'greatness' as a public figure, which makes his physical assault on Desdemona even more astounding and incredible. See examination question 1, page 68.

It is worth noting Desdemona's behaviour throughout this scene – sympathy for her is heightened by her reaction to Othello's disgraceful actions. She remains dutiful and controlled in contrast to Othello who launches into a tirade of abuse against her. Othello orders Desdemona 'Out of my sight!', the irony being that he has completely lost sight of the truth and his perceptions of reality are warped. Othello sees Desdemona's tears as false and her duty and obedience, mentioned three times in this short passage (lines 239–255), as deceitful. Othello's speech again breaks down into passionate confusion and he only manages to regain control of himself for a short time when Desdemona finally is allowed to leave. Othello manages to return to the appropriate formality of address by inviting Lodovico to dine with him that evening, but this is not sustained as he slips into nonsense again as he leaves the stage.

The impact of this incident is devastating. Lodovico, who is left on stage with Iago, reminds the audience of Othello's former high standing in society, emphasising the tragic fall of Othello's character. Iago does not miss an opportunity to twist the knife, condemning Othello and suggesting, again by implication, that Othello is unfit for office.

Act 4, Scene 2

Othello confronts a shocked Desdemona. Iago meets with a disgruntled Roderigo who wishes to know what has been done to further his suit with Desdemona. Iago convinces Roderigo that Cassio must be killed in order to make Othello and Desdemona stay in Cyprus.

'What shall I do to win my Lord again?'

Othello questions Emilia in his desperation to find out any salacious details of the meetings between Cassio and Desdemona, but he is disappointed by Emilia's defence of Desdemona's honour. It is significant how easily Othello dismisses Emilia's support for Desdemona: he is looking for further evidence to condemn Desdemona and does not expect her innocence to be defended so vociferously. By questioning Emilia's honour he can easily dismiss her entreaties. Othello's view of women is now similar to that of Iago, showing how far Iago's influence has permeated Othello's thinking.

Othello attempts to make Desdemona admit her infidelity, but she does not understand the thrust of his questions and protests her innocence. She still believes that it is the orders from Venice that are upsetting Othello, although he subsequently makes it clear to Desdemona that it is her honour that is in question.

Coursework

Note Desdemona's response to Othello's accusations – although dutiful and obedient, she refuses to accept that she has been unfaithful, in spite of Othello's bullying. She shows strength of character in adversity here (see the coursework question on page 64) and is repulsed by Othello's suggestion that she has committed adultery.

It is interesting that Desdemona returns to her faith as a Christian in proving her innocence. Othello, in the style of Iago, twists Desdemona's words and uses them against her. Desdemona reels under Othello's brutal attack and is astonished that Othello, her great love, could possibly hold such an opinion of her.

Iago is sent for by Desdemona to see if he knows the basis for Othello's accusations. It is at this point that Iago's machinations come closest to breaking down. As Desdemona questions Iago, Emilia suggests that Othello has been misinformed by a 'villain' whose intention is to secure promotion. Emilia's perception of the situation is, of course, nearer to the truth than is comfortable for Iago, who attempts to quieten Emilia. Eventually, when Emilia suggests that Iago has had suspicions concerning herself and Othello due to false stories, Iago silences her with an insult, 'You are a fool, go to.' This is a critical moment. Preoccupied with thoughts of her own Desdemona does not react to Emilia's words. Instead, fortunately for him, she turns to Iago for advice.

Desdemona's love for Othello is shown in her appeal to Iago. Rather than being a passive and pathetic figure she wishes to act to prove her innocence.

Love

She kneels and makes an oath that she has never been unfaithful to Othello, which contrasts with Othello's earlier pact to destroy her. She ominously suggests that Othello could take her life but never destroy her love for him. While Othello is prepared, through his own insecurities, to be persuaded that Desdemona has been unfaithful, she shows her constancy, heightening the tragedy of the events that follow. It is significant that in the face of such pure and honest devotion Iago is almost speechless and can only suggest that Othello is concerned with political matters and that everything will turn out fine.

The reappearance of Roderigo

Iago

Just as Iago manages to placate Desdemona another challenge presents itself in the form of Roderigo. Roderigo enters and accuses Iago of duping him. Roderigo has every right to feel aggrieved as we learn that he has given Iago most of his money in order for Iago to arrange a meeting between Roderigo and Desdemona. This is another critical moment in Iago's plans. Roderigo states that he is so dissatisfied that he will reveal himself to Desdemona, ask for his money back and relinquish his suit. Obviously this would lead to Iago's exposure, so he must now use his powers of manipulation to the full. Iago uses Roderigo's outburst to heap praise upon him, suggesting that Roderigo is proving his mettle and that he has legitimate cause to be dissatisfied – Iago effectively dissipates Roderigo's complaints by agreeing with him.

In response to Iago's 'I have dealt most directly in thy affairs,' Roderigo counters 'I do not find that thou deal'st justly with me.' Iago is on the point of being exposed and yet he skilfully manipulates the situation to present Roderigo with the prize he has been waiting for. Iago informs Roderigo that Othello and Desdemona have been instructed to leave Cyprus and that a delay could be created if the newly appointed governor, Cassio, were 'removed'. Roderigo's attack has been pre-empted and he is now drawn into the plot to kill Cassio. He is still uncertain, but Iago has caught his attention and begins to convince him that this is the appropriate course of action if he wishes to enjoy Desdemona. The scene ends with Roderigo requesting further information, but the audience is in no doubt that he is ensnared in Iago's web again. From a position of potential disaster Iago has managed to ensure his own safety and the death of Cassio.

Act 4, Scene 3

Desdemona and Emilia discuss the nature of infidelity.

'She was in love, and he she lov'd prov'd mad...'

Desdemona's constancy and loyalty to Othello, even at this point in the play,

are made explicit to the audience. In spite of his treatment of her, she displays a deep love for Othello which exacerbates the tragic actions of the general in the next act. Desdemona's discussion with Emilia confirms her loyalty to Othello. While Emilia is cynical about relationships Desdemona is true; while Emilia is critical of Othello ('I wish you had never seen him...') Desdemona is constant ('my love doth so approve him.'). Even though Desdemona displays loyalty to Othello in this scene there are still some foreboding thoughts which manifest themselves in her dialogue with Emilia. Desdemona ominously mentions a maid of her mother's called Barbary whose love had gone mad and forsaken her. The maid died singing a song that mirrored her fate, and Desdemona cannot get this song out of her mind. As Desdemona sings this mournful song the audience's sympathy for her is heightened.

Shakespeare is at pains to reveal Desdemona's almost naïve innocence as she asks Emilia if women commit adultery. The effect this has resonates into Act 5 and contrasts with Othello's sordid acceptance of his wife's infidelity. Desdemona's idealistic view of love and constancy clashes with the crude realism of Emilia. Desdemona, it appears, cannot conceive of committing

Love

adultery; Emilia, on the other hand, uses cynical semantics to justify the act of adultery. Emilia then subtly accuses men of forcing women into committing adultery and lists possible causes, such as breaking out into petty jealousies and striking them, both of which Othello and Iago have been guilty of. Emilia champions adultery as a form of revenge. Her language

is reminiscent of Iago's here as she skilfully argues a cynical case for adultery: she insists that women, just like men, have affections, desires for sport and frailties, and so the wrongdoing of men will instruct women to follow suit. Desdemona's response is significant as she still refuses to accept Emilia's line of argument and suggests that women should observe men's weaknesses and learn from their mistakes. Desdemona is prepared to suffer for her love rather than imitate poor behaviour; unfortunately she will ultimately pay for her love with her life.

■ Self-test questions Act 4

Who? What? Why? When? Where? How?

1 Who does Iago convince to murder Cassio?
2 What does Bianca have in her possession which enrages Othello?
3 Why do you think Iago suggests that Othello strangle Desdemona?

4   When does Othello question Emilia about Desdemona and Cassio?
5   Where does Desdemona sing the 'willow' song?
6   How does Lodovico explain Othello's frame of mind?
7   Who is the main subject of the conversation between Cassio and Iago?
8   What time does Iago suggest that Roderigo attack Cassio, and why?
9   How does Desdemona respond to Emilia's view of relationships at the end of Act 4?
10   Where does Iago say that Roderigo will find Cassio?

Who said this, and why?
1   'Oh no, he goes into Mauritania, and takes away with him the fair Desdemona.'
2   'I have not deserved this.'
3   'I took you for that cunning whore of Venice...'
4   'I do not find that thou deal'st justly with me.'
5   'Are his wits safe? Is he not light of brain?'

Prove it!
Provide comment and textual evidence to prove the following.
1   Emilia believes Desdemona is honest.
2   Desdemona begins to fear for her life.
3   Cassio has a low opinion of Bianca.
4   Iago's plot is nearly uncovered, inadvertently, by his wife Emilia.
5   Emilia believes that infidelity is sometimes justified.

Act 5, Scene 1

Cassio is attacked by Roderigo. Roderigo is badly injured and Cassio is wounded surreptitiously by Iago. Iago kills Roderigo and accuses him of being a thief.

'Quick, quick, fear nothing, I'll be at thy elbow...'

Iago's plotting is now coming to fruition. Roderigo, who is clearly

Iago

uncomfortable about attacking Cassio as he fears for his own safety, has been convinced by Iago that Cassio must die. We see how acute Iago's villainy is as he speculates on the outcome of the attack, stating that regardless of who dies he will be able to use the fight to his advantage – he would like Cassio dead, but if Roderigo dies all the money and jewels Iago has taken from him will be secure. Notice Iago's nonchalant and, according to some critics, unconvincing motivation for Cassio's murder. Initially it is Iago's vain and petty jealousy (Cassio's 'daily beauty' making Iago 'ugly') that is the premise for Cassio's death; later, the possibility of Othello revealing Iago's plan to Cassio becomes another motive.

The bungled attempt by Roderigo on Cassio's life is almost comic. Roderigo's cowardly strike is easily deflected by Cassio and it is Roderigo who is wounded. In contrast we see that the villainy of Iago knows no bounds as he, under the cover of darkness, slips into the melee unobserved and wounds Cassio in the leg.

Othello

During the noise and chaos of the ambush on Cassio, Othello enters and takes heart from what he perceives to be Iago's 'honest' and 'brave' behaviour. The dramatic irony is heavy as we have previously witnessed Iago's cowardly behaviour and been privy to his whimsical motivations regarding the destruction of life. Ironically, Othello, sensing that the murder of Cassio is at hand, determines to continue with his half of the hellish pact and murder his wife Desdemona: 'Thy bed, lust stain'd, shall with lust's blood be spotted.'

'O damn'd Iago, O inhuman dog...'

Appearance

Once more Iago skilfully protects his position as he meets with the two Venetian senators, Lodovico and Gratiano, who come to investigate the noise created by the street brawl. Notice the way Shakespeare builds up the speed and tension of the scene by using exclamations and questions. The darkness of the scene is exacerbated by the reticence of the characters. Iago uses this confusion to his advantage as he stumbles upon the wounded Roderigo, accuses him of villainy and the attempted murder of Cassio and executes him. Iago's actions could be construed as heroic as he comes to the rescue of Cassio, but at the same time he is disposing of a potential risk of exposure. Roderigo has served his purpose and is accordingly dispatched. It is interesting to note that Roderigo's final words (line 62) are the first accurate description of Iago we have heard from another character. Unfortunately for Roderigo, and for the other characters, they are unheard and too late. For the first time in the play Iago reveals his true self to another character, with the possible exception of Emilia: there is no way that Iago can allow Roderigo to live if he is to protect his own position.

Iago

Iago cruelly rounds on Bianca, in spite of her obvious distress at Cassio's condition, and again reveals his misogyny by accusing her of playing some part in the attempt on Cassio's life. This, it appears, further protects Iago's own position and in some way discredits Cassio: 'This is the fruits of whoring...'. Iago is firmly in control of the proceedings at this point, and he behaves with exemplary decorum in his exchanges with the two senators. He makes himself appear to be a good man to have around in a crisis when, in fact, unbeknown to everybody else, he has created the chaos in the first place!

Act 5, Scene 2

Othello suffocates Desdemona with a pillow. His murderous act is interrupted by Emilia, whose clamour draws Montano and the others to the scene of the crime. Iago's villainy is finally exposed, and Emilia reveals the truth about the handkerchief. Othello attacks Iago who in turn stabs his wife then flees. Realising his folly and asking for forgiveness Othello takes his own life. Iago is led away and Lodovico returns to Venice to report the news.

'I will kill thee,/And love thee after...'

The scene opens with Othello attempting to justify the action he is about to

Jealousy

take. He feels that he is entitled to kill Desdemona because of her unfaithfulness. He enters the dark bedchamber where Desdemona sleeps carrying a light, and he likens the act of extinguishing the light of the candle with extinguishing Desdemona's life. It is ironic that Othello regains the former poetry of his speech as he prepares to do his most heinous act.

There is further irony when Othello hesitates and questions his actions because Desdemona looks so innocent and pure as she sleeps – of course, she actually is both of these things. Othello is totally blinded by his jealousy, and the bitter twist to his opening speech is that he feels that once Desdemona is dead and has paid for her crimes he will love her again. We are to see later that, once Iago's treachery is revealed, Othello's love does return, but too late.

Imagine the confusion and fear that Desdemona must feel at this stage of the play. She wakes to find the impressive and imposing figure of her husband

Desdemona

looming through the darkness, asking whether she has prayed and has anything to repent as he would not wish to 'kill her soul'. Desdemona senses that she is in mortal danger, but the reason for Othello's wrath is still a mystery to her. She presents us with a vivid description of Othello's demeanour and temperament as she asks 'why gnaw you so your nether lip?'

and sees that, 'Some bloody passion shakes your very frame...'. Othello now returns to the one piece of concrete evidence he feels he has against Desdemona, namely the handkerchief. He is not prepared to accept any of Desdemona's reasons for Cassio's possession of the handkerchief, and the intensity of the scene increases as Othello claims that Cassio has boasted of his illicit relationship with Desdemona. Desdemona pleads with Othello to ask Cassio to speak the truth, and he responds by informing her that Cassio's death has been seen to by Iago. In a moment of lucidity Desdemona realises Iago's villainy ('My fear interprets then...') and understands that Cassio 'is betray'd, and I undone.' The pitch of the scene intensifies as Desdemona begs for her life, but Othello resolutely stifles her.

Coursework

'And yet I fear you' (5.2, line 37). Desdemona's reaction to Othello is painfully realistic. She realises she is in grave danger and her terror is made explicit. The way she begs for her life lines 79–83 is both moving and tragic (see the coursework question, page 64).

'And sweet revenge grows harsh...'

Othello's next speech (lines 92–102) is disjointed and broken, reflecting his state of mind. Emilia enters to bring the news of Roderigo's death and Cassio's injury, and in this instant Desdemona rouses herself from the brink of death and her cry, 'O, falsely, falsely murdered!' reflects the attempt on Cassio's life and reinforces the tragic actions of Othello. Desdemona's love and loyalty are true to the end: her final words are uttered to protect her husband and reveal the depth of her love for him.

Othello

However, Othello, blinded by his lust for revenge, still cannot see the truth; he twists Desdemona's heroic and poignant gesture and uses it as further proof of her capacity for deception as she dies uttering an untruth – he is, indeed, the murderer.

Revenge

Othello tells Emilia that the originator of his murderous actions has been Iago – in attempting to justify his actions Othello begins to unravel Iago's plotting.

Coursework

'Nobody, I myself, farewell' (5.2, line 125). Is this an incredible response or Desdemona's ultimate proof of her deep love for Othello? Even in death she attempts to protect her husband, an ultimate act of self-sacrifice which reverberates with poignancy (see the coursework question on page 64).

The irony of the line 'My friend, thy husband, honest, honest Iago' is explicit and reinforces Othello's tragic misconception. Emilia's confidence in Desdemona's honesty and the sense of justice she feels must be done enables her to overcome her fear of Othello and draw attention to the scene of the crime by shouting for help and accusing Othello of murder.

Coursework

It is worth noting Emilia's reaction to the accusation that Desdemona has been unfaithful (see the coursework question on page 64). She is adamant in her condemnation of Othello and unquestioning in her loyalty to and faith in Desdemona. Emilia is shocked by the thought that Iago has cast such aspersions on Desdemona (look at the way she repeats in disbelief, 'My husband?'), but she ultimately acknowledges that he has the capacity for such villainy and she places Desdemona's fidelity above her own husband's honesty.

There is some irony in the fact that it is Emilia, Iago's own wife, who finally exposes his villainy. It is interesting that Iago has managed to mask his true self even from his wife until now. Emilia, in line 175, questions Othello's

Appearance

accusations of her husband; she asks Iago to refute the words of Othello and deny that he had any part in suggesting Desdemona had been unfaithful, 'I know thou didst not, thou art not such a villain...'. Once Iago, coldly and concisely, confirms Othello's words Emilia exclaims 'You told a lie, an odious damn'd lie...', and Iago's plan begins to crumble. Emilia's distress and rage is voluble and convincing, so Iago attempts to silence her. As she realises Iago's villainy Emilia also acknowledges her own part in Desdemona's downfall. Her decision to turn against her own husband whom, as she says, she is duty bound to obey, is a decision that Iago did not anticipate. The handkerchief has been the crucial piece of evidence used by Iago to convince Othello of Desdemona's dishonesty, and when Othello mentions this Iago realises that his scheme is on the point of discovery. In line 220, the speech beginning ''Twill out, it will...' indicates a linguistic shift of power: Iago, who has manipulated all of the characters through his skilful use of language prior to this, is now undone by the direct and arguably heroic testimony of his own wife. As the secret of the handkerchief is revealed Iago's mask slips and he draws his sword against his own wife. Othello comes to a sudden realisation and launches himself at Iago who, in the melee, stabs Emilia and flees.

'Moor she was chaste, she lov'd thee, cruel Moor...'

As the tragic events unravel Othello finally begins to realise that his actions

Love

have been fatally unjust and he acknowledges his loss. He claims that he has been ill-fated and, therefore, almost powerless to stop himself from committing this tragic act of murder, but he understands that he must pay the price. Othello perceives that he has lost all sense of himself and he wishes upon himself eternal damnation for his crime. The love that he has for Desdemona floods back and it is the realisation of what he has destroyed that will ultimately bring about his own destruction.

Examination

When answering examination question 1, page 68, consider Othello's speech starting on line 260. Does he regain some of the dignity which he has lost? Is his sorrow convincing? Is this proof of his 'greatness of heart'?

Iago

Iago's villainy is made complete at the end of the play when he refuses to give Othello the small comfort of understanding the motivation for his lies and crimes: 'Demand me nothing, what you know, you know,/From this time forth I never will speak word.' There is no final redemption for Iago as there is for Edmund in *King Lear*, and he does not pay for his crimes with his life, even though Othello attempts to kill him. Iago's refusal to speak is his final twist of the knife; the character whose language has done so much damage now refuses to speak: this is arguably Iago's ultimate, stubborn victory. He is taken off to prison to face incarceration and torture at the very least. Do you think Iago 'wins' in the end? What is your final assessment of his character? What do you think motivated him to bring about Othello's destruction?

Othello's final speech is complex. Obviously, because of his actions, he is disgraced – Lodovico removes control of Cyprus from the general and transfers it to Cassio. Othello then requests that he be allowed to speak, and he reminds those gathered that his service to Venice must allow him this appeal. Othello's speech is once again rich with poetry, and he restores some of his former dignity and honour. The jealous and unreasonable general, intent on revenge for his damaged pride at any cost, disappears and the eloquent, proud and dignified Othello who we had seen at the opening of the play begins to re-emerge. His concern is that the truth is heard when this tragic story is retold: 'then you must speak,/Of one that lov'd not wisely, but too well...'. Othello assumes his former dignity by admitting his mistakes while protesting his love for Desdemona. The pathos of this final speech is unquestionable as he likens the loss of Desdemona to a pearl being cast away in ignorance by a 'base Indian'. His story of the Turk who threatened the State of Venice is analogous with his current situation, and the sentence which he carried out on the Turk he now carries out on himself. Othello's suicide restores some of his dignity, yet leaves the audience with a sense of real loss and waste: the tragedy is complete.

Iago is taken away to prison and Lodovico resolves, with a heavy heart, to travel back to Venice and inform the Duke of the tragic occurrences.

At the end do you see Othello as 'great of heart' as Cassio describes him? Or is his final speech riddled with insecurities as he attempts to convince the state, with his story of killing the Turk, that he has been a faithful servant? What is your final view of Othello?

◼ Self-test questions Act 5

Who? What? Why? When? Where? How?

1   Who does Iago murder first?
2   What does Iago refuse to do after he is arrested?
3   Why is Iago led away to be tortured?
4   When Desdemona dies what does she do to protect Othello?
5   Where does Othello die?

6 How does Othello describe his love for Desdemona at the end of the play?
7 Who takes over from Othello as Governor of Cyprus?
8 What action finally uncovers Iago's villainy?
9 How does Othello die?
10 Where does Lodovico return and why?

Who said this, and why?
1 'My husband?'
2 'O damn'd Iago, O inhuman dog ... oh, oh, oh.'
3 'He has a daily beauty in his life,/That makes me ugly...'
4 ' 'Twill out, it will: I hold my peace sir, no...'
5 'I have done the state some service, and they know't...'

Prove it!
1 Iago is unrepentant.
2 Desdemona's love for Othello never falters.
3 Desdemona knows that Othello is going to kill her.
4 Othello's death will be a loss to the State of Venice.
5 Othello asks for forgiveness.

How to write a coursework essay

Different examining boards have different requirements for A Level coursework, but there are certain principles that hold good in every case. We will consider these and also a possible title for coursework. However, essays can not only be of *different lengths*, but of *different types*. You are probably most likely to find yourself writing on one text (approximately 1,500–2,000 words), comparing two texts (3,000 words) or writing about a literary genre referring to at least three texts (up to 5,000 words). Most of these word-length requirements are optional maximums; *it is essential that you check with your teacher that there is no penalty for extra length.*

If you are choosing a *comparative* title, you must make sure that comparisons are made throughout, not necessarily in the same sentence, but at least in adjacent paragraphs. Your essay title must direct you to some specific comparison, not just a generalised survey of similarities and differences. Remember also that 'comparison' always implies 'contrast' as well – discussing different ways of approaching a theme, plot-line or genre can always be productive.

The single-text coursework essay is in many ways similar. A specific task is again essential, and once again your theme or line of argument must be kept before the reader throughout. Narration is almost always unhelpful: even at A Level, 'telling the story' is the most common failing. Almost equally dangerous is taking opinions from critics without fully understanding them and failing to absorb them into your arguments. *Copying* from critics without acknowledgement is, of course, plagiarism and can result in disqualification.

The need for a developing argument or comparison has implications for your method of approaching the essay. You should make general notes on the material (textual evidence, useful quotations, comments by critics, etc.), then shape them into an ordered framework (probably simply by numbering them in an appropriate order) before working through at least two or three drafts of the essay. You should be fully aware of what each paragraph is to be about, as far as possible signalling this to the reader in the first sentence, often called the *topic sentence* for this reason. With comparatively short essays like these, you should make sure that your style is concise and time is not wasted on unnecessary quotations. Relevant, fairly brief quotations are very valuable, absorbed into your sentences if very short, or set out on separate lines if slightly longer. It is unlikely that quotations of more than a few lines will really help you.

The actual presentation of your essay is also important. With coursework it is sheer carelessness to make errors in spelling, punctuation or syntax or (worst of all) to confuse or misspell characters' names. Unless there is a definite reason for doing so, avoid slang and colloquialisms, including contractions like 'they've' for 'they have'.

The format of introduction–essay–conclusion is perfectly acceptable but, used over-formally, can weight the essay too much in the direction of semi-relevant generalisation at the beginning and the end. In a good essay, the conclusion will simply be the final stage of a developed argument.

The example title given below can be easily adapted to a comparative essay with another text(s). Use the outline to form your notes on this text. The points should also help you to focus your approach to the other text(s).

An *outline* of a model answer has been supplied for the essay title below. Use this outline in conjunction with material in the **Who's who**, **Themes and ideas** and **Text commentary sections** of this guide. In addition, the points raised as Examiner's tips throughout the Text commentary should prove particularly useful.

'The women in Othello *lack power and importance; they are used purely as dramatic devices to offset the tragedy of the main character.' How far would you agree with this statement?*

It would be feasible for you to agree with the statement if you could find substantial evidence to construct a coherent argument and back up your point with references to the text. However, hopefully you would take issue with this statement and attempt to disprove it by focusing on the three women presented in the play. By analysing each character in depth and detail you would be able to show that the women in the play do function as characters in their own right and that they are not merely passive and disempowered dramatic devices.

Desdemona, for example, is often misinterpreted as solely a foil for Othello's jealousy. While there is no doubting that Desdemona is supposed to be perceived as a good character she does reveal complexities in her nature that are worth considering and highlighting.

An analysis of Desdemona's character should include:

- the way she rebels against her father and convention by marrying Othello;
- her public declaration of love for Othello (Act 1, Scene 3);
- her intellect and wit shown through her conversation with Iago (Act 2, Scene 1);
- her willingness to help others, such as Cassio (Act 3, Scene 3);
- her tenacity in maintaining her innocence;

- her fear of Othello and her subsequent loyalty to him (Act 5, Scene 2);
- her love for Othello throughout the play.

By focusing on these points you will be able to construct a convincing argument regarding Desdemona's credibility as a character.

Emilia, too, is by no means a mere spectator in the play, and ultimately it is she who uncovers her husband's villainous plotting. Her character is developed and, as the play progresses, her role and contribution become very significant.

An analysis of Emilia's character should include:

- her role in convincing Desdemona to help Cassio;
- her mistake in giving Iago the handkerchief;
- her perception in sensing Othello's jealousy (Act 3, Scene 4);
- her fierce loyalty to Desdemona (Act 4, Scene 2);
- her cynical, yet realistic, view of relationships (Act 4, Scene 3);
- the way she stands up to Othello (Act 5, Scene 2);
- her part in the revelation of Iago's villainy.

Bianca, Cassio's mistress, is also worth mentioning. Even though she is a minor character and her reputation is dubious she does display a commitment to Cassio. Her jealousy concerning the handkerchief mirrors Othello's jealousy in the sense that it is equally groundless, and she shows that she is prepared to face humiliation in her quest for Cassio's love.

It can be concluded, therefore, that the women in the text play an integral part in developing and furthering the plot, even though they are defined by their relationships with others. Shakespeare's skill is shown by the way he clearly presents all the women in the play as believable and convincing individuals.

How to write an examination essay

Preparation

- The *first essential* is thorough revision. You may be answering questions in either a traditional examination or an Open Book examination. It is vital that you remember that in an Open Book examination you have enough time to look up quotations and references, but *only if you know where to look*.

- The revision process should begin well before the examination: a matter of months rather than weeks. Initially you need to re-read texts, which is not a good idea the week before the examination. It is then useful to make notes, both to assist memory at the time and to provide a summary for later revision. These notes should be arranged to give a pattern to your study: by themes, characters, techniques, etc. Quotations should not be learned simply by rote, but together with relevant uses for them. A late stage of revision should be to fix the patterns of knowledge in your mind, probably by writing practice essays.

- The time process is very important – trying to absorb new material the night before the examination is likely to be positively harmful.

Before you start writing

- Read the questions very carefully, both to choose the most suitable title and to be certain of exactly what you are asked to do. It is very easy, but potentially disastrous, to answer the essay you *hope or imagine* has been asked, or to reproduce a practice essay you wrote on a vaguely similar theme.

- A Level questions need careful attention. Do not respond instantly to a quotation without checking what the question asks you to write about it. Make certain that you are aware of every part of a question: many ask you to do two or three distinct things, and omitting one of these immediately reduces your possible marks. Check for words like compare, contrast, analyse, consider and discuss.

- You do not have much spare time in an examination, but it is worthwhile spending a few minutes noting down the material you think is relevant, matching it with the instructions you have been given and drawing up an essay plan. Starting on the wrong essay or starting the right one in the wrong way ultimately wastes time.

- Make sure that your plan develops a consistent argument or point of view – you will not be asked to tell the story, and essays that take a chronological approach seldom do well.

Writing the essay

- The first sentences are very important. You should begin the essay by informing the examiner of the opinion you are going to develop, the contrasts you are going to study, or your view of the problem you are about to analyse. This should stay in focus throughout the essay – if possible, each paragraph should begin with a topic sentence relating the material of that paragraph to your overall theme or argument.

- Do not spend too long introducing the essay: move quickly to the material you wish to cover. Throughout, check your plan to make sure that you deal with all the points you wish to make.

- Quotation is particularly relevant where the style of expression is important in itself or in revealing character or the author's viewpoint. It is less important when you are referring to events. Quotations should be kept fairly short and should be relevant, not simply attractive or well known. In many cases it is possible to absorb a quotation into your sentence, but quotations of a few lines must be set out separately and as in the text.

- There is no 'correct' length for an essay. The fact that someone else is clearly writing huge amounts does not mean that he or she will obtain better marks than you. However, you should make sure that you use your time fully, write concisely and avoid padding.

- It is dangerous to exceed the allotted time for each question by more than a few minutes, especially as marks can always be gained most easily at the start of an essay. Make sure that you tackle the required number of questions. For this reason, though an elegant conclusion is desirable, it may sometimes be necessary to omit it.

- Examiners understand that candidates are writing under pressure, but it is still important that you maintain as high a standard of written expression as possible. Avoid slang, colloquialisms and contractions (e.g. 'they've' for 'they have') wherever possible.

- Examination questions inevitably invite the candidate to present an argument. Decide on your position and make sure that you refer to both sides of the argument. Whether the question pertains to a theme or a specific scene in the text, you must demonstrate your knowledge of the whole text. Make sure that you refer to specific examples throughout the play in your argument.

An *outline* of a model answer has been supplied for each essay title below. Use this outline in conjunction with material in the **Who's who**, **Themes and ideas** and **Text commentary** sections of this guide. In addition, the points raised as Examiner's tips throughout the Text commentary should prove particularly useful.

1. *'For he was great of heart.'* How far would you agree with Cassio's assessment of Othello?

- Any discussion of Othello's character will inevitably lead you to the nature of the tragic hero in Shakespeare's plays. An assessment and analysis of Othello's role in the play, how he is viewed by other characters and the motivation for his actions must be addressed if you wish to answer this question fully. Cassio has been wronged by Othello, yet he acknowledges the tragic nature of Othello's demise by his direct and poignant statement.

- There is no doubt that Othello experiences some kind of 'fall' from a position of great respect and responsibility to that of an envy-ridden murderer who loses all sense of himself, only to regain some of his esteem in his final speeches and actions. If you chart the development of Othello there is much evidence at the beginning of the play to suggest that he is a capable and important figure on the political stage in Venice. He is confident and deals with the fury of Brabantio in a calm and sophisticated manner. You may feel that Othello displays signs of over-confidence in his worth to the State of Venice by the complacent way he agrees to answer Brabantio's accusations, but you could point out that he is prepared to accept the judgement of the Duke and graciously and publicly defends his love for Desdemona, showing the his depth of feeling for her, and proving that he is prepared to do anything, even jeopardise his own position, to secure her love.

- Othello's greatness of heart is shown predominantly at the beginning of the play and is realised through his love for Desdemona. Desdemona draws out a side of Othello's character that reveals his capacity to love (see Act 1, Scene 3, line 120 onwards and Act 2, Scene 1 line 180 onwards). That Othello loves Desdemona is never in question, so what is it that prompts such a turnabout in his whole manner and view of the world? In short, Iago. Whatever Othello's weaknesses, such as his pride and his insecurity because of his race, it is the way in which Iago exploits Othello's nature which is the single most powerful factor in bringing about the tragic outcome of the play. As Iago states, Othello has an open nature and is therefore susceptible to exploitation.

- The private and public sides of Othello's nature are very different – Iago discerns this and takes advantage of it. Othello is a confident soldier, brave and determined, but as a lover he is less confident and riddled with insecurity. It seems that Othello is not an unreasonably jealous man like Leontes in *A Winter's Tale*, but he falls victim to the disease of jealousy thanks to Iago's skilled manipulation.

- Once Othello falls victim to the suggestions of Iago he begins to lose his 'greatness', for example, you could examine the way that his use of language changes. At the opening of the play Othello is shown to be eloquent, his speech possessing rich imagery and poetry (see Act 1, Scene 3), yet by Act 3, Scene 3 his language is broken and lacking in control as jealousy pervades his mind.

- Othello seems to lose the sense of his true self, and as he degenerates his nature changes. He begins to harbour thoughts of revenge and murder, losing control to such an extent that he strikes Desdemona in public. As Othello plummets he becomes more and more blind to the truth and cannot see Desdemona's obvious innocence.

- It is only at the end of the play when Othello realises he has been tragically misled that he begins to redeem himself and restore some of the 'greatness' of character that he showed at the beginning of the play. His suicide is necessary if he is to be defined as a tragic hero: he acknowledges his mistakes and his capacity to err and determines to join his love, Desdemona, in death. His final speech, which also serves as an epitaph, recaptures his past eloquence and the pathos of his words emphasises the dreadful sense of loss and waste we witness at the end of the play. If you cannot accept Othello as being 'great of heart' it is very difficult to accept *Othello* as a tragedy.

2. *'The plotting of Iago is both incredible and without substance.' What is your view of the way Iago is presented in Othello?*

- Iago is possibly the most intriguing, complex and evil of all Shakespeare's villains. At the opening of the play we see him having a conversation with Roderigo in which he declares his dissatisfaction with his master, Othello. He clearly states that he is keen to disrupt the life of Othello and that of his new lieutenant, Cassio, because he has been overlooked for promotion. This question, however, is asking you to consider two things: firstly, whether Iago's plotting is convincing, and secondly, if he has any credible motivation for his actions.

- Iago's skill as a manipulator can be seen very early on in the play, during Act 1, Scene 1 as he manages, after Roderigo's feeble attempts, to convince Brabantio that Othello has stolen his daughter Desdemona. Iago focuses crudely on the sexual activity of Othello and Desdemona and suggests that they are at that moment 'making the beast with two backs': it is graphic imagery like this which stirs Brabantio into action.

- As the play continues it is clear that Iago's initial motivation for revenge is his annoyance at being passed over for promotion in favour of Cassio, who he feels is not a capable soldier and has only been promoted because he is Othello's friend. Iago's pragmatic plan of revenge starts from this premise and grows into a skilfully intricate plot.

- Another motive that is revealed is that Iago's hatred for Othello comes from a suspicion that Othello has had an affair with Emilia, Iago's wife. At first this seems to be a whimsical excuse from Iago to justify the intensity of his revenge, but Emilia herself later confirms that a rumour to this effect has been circulating (Act 4, Scene 2). She denies the rumour fiercely, but it gives Iago legitimate motivation for his actions.

- The skill of Iago's plotting is seen in the downfall of Cassio. Iago expertly manipulates all of the characters: he convinces Roderigo to aid him in his plan; he manages to persuade Cassio to drink; and he even prejudices Montano against the lieutenant. The success of the plot relies purely on the pragmatic skills of Iago as he responds to opportunity, driving towards his ultimate goal – the destruction of Othello. Iago's motivation now seems to be his delight in control and power. He feels he should be in a higher position than he is, and he proves his worth by manipulating all of the other characters. It is power that now seems to be the factor that determines his actions.

- Iago's power over other characters is portrayed most convincingly through his control over Othello. Through his linguistic powers of persuasion and intimation Iago focuses on and manipulates Othello's weaknesses and vulnerabilities. In Act 3, Scene 3 Iago moves from suggestion to doubt to accusation and skilfully carries the naïve general along with him. By the time Iago provides 'ocular proof', Othello has already convinced himself of Desdemona's infidelity. Othello's lack of self-knowledge enables him to be blinded by the truth, and he is convinced of Iago's honesty. While the constraints of the dramatic form make it difficult to suggest the passing of time, Iago's exploitation of Othello is expertly handled (see the Arden introduction for an interesting examination of the 'double time scheme').

- Ultimately, Iago's real mystery as a villain is maintained by his reluctance to confess and his vow of silence at the end of the play. However, to view Iago as an inhuman dramatic device who acts without motive or credibility is to misunderstand one of Shakespeare's greatest human villains.

Self-test answers Act 1

Who? What? Why? When? Where? How?

1   Iago. It shows his duplicity in the play – he makes it clear that he is intent on appearing loyal to Othello so that he can destroy him.

2   He initially uses the image of theft to rouse Brabantio, then he uses overt sexual references to inflame Brabantio's anger.

3   Because of the imminent attack of the Turkish fleet on Cyprus. This shows Othello's importance to the state.

4   When he visited Brabantio's house and told stories about his life.

5   To Cyprus to protect the island from assault by the Turks.

6   Iago is twenty-eight: 'I have looked upon the world for four times seven years...' (1.3, line 308).

7   Othello is referring to Iago. It is ironic as Iago is planning Othello's downfall.

8   He will ensure Roderigo wins Desdemona if he provides Iago with money and jewels to bribe her.

9   Florence: 'One Michael Cassio, a Florentine...'

10 At the end of Act 1. It shows that Iago is clearly using Roderigo and that he is intent on bringing about the downfall of both Othello and Cassio. His plan for revenge is still in its infancy, but he already ruminates upon engendering jealous thoughts in the mind of the general concerning the fidelity of his lieutenant, Michael Cassio, and his wife, Desdemona.

Who said this, and why?

1   The Duke says this after hearing of how Desdemona fell in love with Othello when listening to his romantic tales of his past exploits. The Duke is subtly and significantly lending his support to Othello as he needs his services in the conflict with Turkey.

2   Brabantio, accusing Othello of stealing his daughter. Desdemona is viewed by Brabantio as a possession to be given away with her father's consent. Interestingly Brabantio echoes the influential and emotive words previously used by Iago.

3   Iago uses these words to shock Brabantio into belief and action. Roderigo's appeals to Brabantio are weak and unheeded, but Iago's explicit sexual references soon focus Brabantio's attention.

4   Othello says this, revealing his insecurity about language and the deeper insecurity about his acceptance by Venetian society. The irony is that Othello, in the speech that follows and at other points of the play, uses some of the most eloquent language spoken in the text.

5   Desdemona says this as she confirms her decision to marry Othello without parental consent. This is an example of Desdemona's maturity, strength and love for Othello.

6   Iago says this when he decides to attempt to destroy Othello, and Cassio in the process, by inspiring jealous thoughts in the general's mind.

Prove it!

1   Cassio, in Act 1, Scene 2 arrives with the news that Othello is required 'post-haste' by the Duke because of the potential conflict with the Turkish forces. It is clear from this point onwards that Othello is confident of the Duke's need for his skills as a general.

2   After Brabantio warns Othello that Desdemona has deceived her father and may well deceive her husband Othello replies with, 'My life upon her faith...'.

3   Iago repeats this several times to Roderigo, but it is only when he soliloquises at the end of the act that we see Iago's unadulterated feelings for the general. Not only has Iago been passed over for promotion, but he fears that Othello has cuckolded him: 'I hate the Moor,/And it is thought abroad that 'twixt my sheets/H'as done my office.' This accusation is unfounded but clearly shows Iago's contempt for Othello.

4   Act 1, Scene 3 presents us with indisputable evidence that Iago is using Roderigo and extorting money from him. The repetition of the instruction to Roderigo to put money in his purse is emphatic in confirming Iago's intentions which are given further credence by his words, 'Thus do I ever make my fool my purse...'.

5   Othello's stories have provided the first spark of love between himself and Desdemona, and when he relates this to the Duke he concedes that Othello's prowess as a storyteller would 'win my daughter too.'

6   There are numerous examples of Desdemona's love for Othello in Act 1. Two distinct examples come in Act 1, Scene 3. Firstly, she publicly declares her love for Othello in spite of her father's disapproval, and secondly she requests that she be allowed to travel with her husband into a potential war zone when he is dispatched to Cyprus.

■ Self-test answers Act 2

Who? What? Why? When? Where? How?

1   Cassio's.

2   He greets both Desdemona and Emilia with chivalrous courtesy. He kneels to Desdemona and kisses Emilia.

3   To celebrate his marriage to Desdemona and the defeat of the Turkish fleet in the storm.

4   Iago suggests the watch begins between ten and eleven o'clock.

5   Iago sends Roderigo after the drunken Cassio to provoke a fight with him.

6   He says they ought to celebrate the marriage of Othello and Desdemona and he encourages Cassio to drink when Montano and other gentlemen arrive.

7   Iago, so that he can begin to suggest that Cassio's behaviour is improper. The secretive nature of Cassio's request gives Iago's suggestions increased validity.

8   He claims that Othello and Desdemona are preparing to leave Cyprus and that only a scandal will keep them there for Roderigo to satisfy his lust.

9   He is seriously wounded and has difficulty speaking.

10   He will ask Emilia, who is close to Desdemona, to encourage her mistress to support Cassio.

Who said this, and why?

1   Cassio says this in the aftermath of the drunken brawl in the streets of Cyprus in which he has been an aggressor. He feels that he has lost his good name because of his behaviour.

2   This is Othello's protestation of love just after he arrives safely in Cyprus. It shows the depth and intensity of his love for Desdemona.

3   Iago says this while plotting to use Cassio's courtly manners to draw him into his plan and bring about his destruction.

4   Othello says this when reluctantly dismissing his friend and lieutenant from public office because of his involvement in the fight.

5   Iago, this time plotting to use Desdemona's 'goodness' to further his villainous machinations. He is certain that she will agree to help Cassio because she is compassionate.

Prove it!

1   Iago plans to use Emilia's position and any influence she may have over Desdemona: 'My wife must move for Cassio to her mistress...' (2.3, line 373).

2   At the beginning of Act 2 we receive confirmation that the Turkish fleet has been destroyed by the stormy weather (lines 19–23).

3   We see this in his conversation with Montano and the gentlemen before Desdemona arrives, and in his reaction when she arrives.

4   In Act 2, Scene 1, from line 100 onwards Iago gives his view of women, which is extremely crude and derogatory but which he dresses up as light-hearted banter. He repeats his low opinion of women in his exchanges with Roderigo (2.1, lines 220–280) and later with Cassio when he speaks crudely of Desdemona (2.3, lines 12–26).

5   In Act 1, Scene 1 when Othello arrives in Cyprus he reveals the depth of his love for Desdemona and his contentment (line 180 onwards). The future appears bright for the newlyweds, although there is some dramatic irony in the line, 'If it were now to die,/'Twere now to be most happy...'. Later in the scene Othello remarks, 'Honey, you shall be well desired in Cyprus,' showing that he anticipates their time on the island will be agreeable.

■ Self-test answers Act 3

Who? What? Why? When? Where? How?

1   Emilia

2   He sends a message to Emilia asking her to press his case with Desdemona.

3   For two reasons: firstly, Cassio has not visited her for a week, and secondly, she suspects that the handkerchief in Cassio's possession is a love token from another admirer.

4   At the beginning of Act 3 he and Othello enter to see Cassio leaving after a meeting with Desdemona. Iago uses the opportunity to suggest that the meeting has been less than innocent with 'Ha! I like not that', and the corruption of Othello's mind begins.

5   In Cassio's lodgings.

6   No more than three days.

7   His mother.

8   Iago describes jealousy as a 'green-ey'd monster'.

9   Iago has seen Othello remain calm in the midst of battle and never get angry even when he has lost men from his own forces.

10 At the beginning of their relationship – it was his first token of love for Desdemona.

Who said this, and why?

1   Desdemona assures Cassio that she will plead his case. She realises that a rift has emerged between Othello and his friend and wishes to restore them to their former friendship.

2   Iago says this to Othello as Cassio leaves Desdemona after asking for her help. He wants to make Othello suspicious of the relationship between Cassio and Desdemona.

3   Othello says this to Iago after the ensign has revealed his suspicions of the relationship between Cassio and Desdemona. Othello feels that Iago's apparent loyalty deserves loyalty in return.
4   Emilia says this. It seems that she will gain Iago's favour by providing him with the handkerchief that he 'hath a hundred times/woo'd me to steal…'.
5   Cassio shows disdain for Bianca when she suggests that the handkerchief he has in his possession is from another mistress.

Prove it!
1   Once Desdemona agrees to help Cassio she shows a constancy and resolve to his case, for example, in Act 3, Scene 3 she assures him that she will do everything in her power to restore his friendship with Othello: 'If I do vow a friendship, I'll perform it/To the last article.'
2   There are numerous examples of Othello's misplaced trust in Iago in this act. When Iago initially voices his suspicions of Cassio Othello is quick to confirm his trust in Iago: 'I know thou art full of love and honesty…' (3.3). There are many more examples, particularly in Act 3, Scene 3 where Othello repeats his trust in Iago's honesty.
3   In Act 3, Scene 3 he is extremely brusque, even hostile, towards Emilia from line 304 onwards. Eventually she gives him Desdemona's handkerchief, obviously trying to attain some approval from him. Once she has given him the handkerchief he is as cold towards her as before.
4   The lines 'I'll tear her all to pieces' and 'O, blood, Iago, blood!' are clear evidence that Othello's thoughts are turning towards murderous revenge.
5   After the dramatic tension of Act 2, which has seen Cassio lose his position and Iago determine upon a course of action which will bring about the destruction of the main characters, the introduction of the clown relieves the tension momentarily with his ambiguous and seemingly crude puns about wind instruments. It gives the audience some respite and allows them to prepare for the even greater tension of the pivotal scene of the play, Act 3, Scene 3.

■ Self-test answers Act 4

Who? What? Why? When? Where? How?
1   Roderigo
2   Desdemona's handkerchief.
3   Othello's original request for Iago to procure some poison with which to kill Desdemona would implicate Iago in the murder, a risk he is unwilling to take. He wants to destroy Othello and get away with it!
4   In Scene 2, just after he has struck Desdemona in public (4.1).
5   In her bedchamber as she prepares for bed.
6   He suggests it might be as a result of the news that Othello has to relinquish his position and return to Venice.
7   Bianca, although Othello believes they are discussing Desdemona.
8   When Cassio leave's Bianca's lodging between midnight and one o'clock. In the dark it will be easy for Roderigo to ambush Cassio.
9   Desdemona is not convinced of Emilia's cynical view of relationships. This is yet another proof of her constancy and fidelity.
10 At Bianca's lodging.

Who said this, and why?

1   Iago uses this lie to convince Roderigo that Cassio must be killed so that Othello will be forced to stay on Cyprus.
2   Desdemona, in response to Othello's physical assault on her.
3   This is Othello's view of Desdemona, which is so distorted that he can only see what Iago has made him believe.
4   Roderigo, finally questioning his treatment by Iago. He feels aggrieved that he has got no closer to Desdemona in spite of all the money and jewels he has given Iago.
5   This is Lodovico's response after witnessing Othello's attack on Desdemona. Remember, Othello has previously been viewed as a disciplined and effective general.

Prove it!

1   At the beginning of Act 4, Scene 1 when Othello questions her about Desdemona's conduct she is resolute and direct, 'I durst, my Lord, to wager she is honest,/Lay down my soul at stake...'
2   She begins to sense that something is seriously wrong in Act 4, Scene 3. She begins to dwell upon morbid thoughts ('If I do die before thee, prithee shroud me/In one of those same sheets' – 4.3, lines 24–25) which are reflected in the story of the 'willow' song.
3   In Scene 1 when Iago questions Cassio about his relationship with Bianca Cassio is quite scathing of her reputation and mocks her love for him (line 105 onwards).
4   Emilia suggests to Othello, at the beginning of Scene 2, that his suspicions have been put in his head by 'a wretch'. She continues this line of argument to Desdemona when, ironically, Iago is present, 'I will be hang'd, if some eternal villain,/Have not devis'd this slander...'
5   At the very end of Act 4 Emilia attempts to put infidelity into perspective and suggests that if men engage in the pursuit then so should women (4.3, lines 84–103).

◼ Self-test answers Act 5

Who? What? Why? When? Where? How?

1   Roderigo.
2   He refuses to justify his actions and says he will never confess: 'From this time forth I never will speak word.'
3   To make him speak.
4   She refuses to implicate him as the murderer.
5   He dies 'upon a kiss', holding Desdemona on her deathbed.
6   He says he loved her 'not wisely, but too well.'
7   Cassio.
8   His stabbing of Emilia to silence her.
9   He stabs himself.
10 He returns to Venice to relate the sad story of Othello to the Duke and his court.

Who said this, and why?

1   Emilia says this when Othello tells her that it was Iago who suggested that Desdemona has been unfaithful: she is obviously shocked and initially refuses to believe Othello.

2   Roderigo's final words when he realises Iago's villainy.

3   Iago says this in a feeble attempt to justify the murder of Cassio.

4   Emilia says this. She is intent on revealing Iago's part in the downfall of her mistress.

5   Othello reminds the people gathered of his importance to the Venetian State and requests they listen carefully to his explanation.

Prove it!

1   Iago's final words are haunting and chilling. He refuses to justify his actions and chooses to remain silent forever (5.2, lines 304–305).

2   Even when she is on the point of death she still wishes to protect Othello by denying that he is her murderer.

3   In Act 5, Scene 2 she begs Othello for a stay of execution – she is clearly aware that her life is in danger, 'Kill me tomorrow, let me live to-night.'

4   There is no doubt of Othello's importance to the State of Venice throughout the play. Lodovico's tone in the final speech of the play reiterates that Othello will be a loss to Venice 'and to the state/This heavy act with heavy heart relate.'

5   Othello's words are poignant and full of pathos. He attempts to suggest that he has acted foolishly but honourably, 'for nought I did in hate, but all in honour' (5.2, line 296), and he asks Cassio directly for forgiveness: 'I ask your pardon' (5.2, line 301).

Notes

Pathos ?

Epitaph

Act 4 scene 2   Emilia Rumour

Notes

Notes

Notes